Where the Past Is Still Happening

To Pat + Kathy,

God Bless You!

Amy Marshall *2021*

ISBN 978-1-0980-9935-0 (paperback)
ISBN 978-1-0980-9936-7 (digital)

Christian Faith Publishing, Inc.
832 Park Avenue
Meadville, PA 16335
www.christianfaithpublishing.com

Printed in the United States of America

For my grandson, Nihon, so that he can know me.

CONTENTS

PREFACE

As we age, the past does not grow dim. In fact, it grows brighter, eventually even brighter than the present. It seems to me that the future is totally dark and the present is murky, but the past is brightly and often warmly lit. We best like to recollect scenes from our lives with others who actually shared or witnessed them. Second to that, we savor these scenes through the telling to others. When a relationship ends or someone dies who has been a life witness, that loss is what we mourn the most.

Every story in this book really happened. Many of them I lived. Others were told to me by the people who lived them. A few were told to my elders when they were young, who in turn, told them to me.

As a child, I kept a barefoot and routine circuit visiting elderly neighbors. Almost everyone who lived on Harmony Road back in the 1950s had been there since the previous century. They traded cookies and milk for a song or two on their old pianos and the pleasure they took in telling me, each time I came around, what they remembered about the town, the times, my house.

I would notice a certain look appear on each elderly face, a sound in each tender voice when they time-traveled with me. I was becoming a witness to their memories. They were giving me these stories the way I am now giving them to you. In some wonderful way, in the telling, we feel as though the past is still happening.

Acknowledgment

Thank you to my dear husband, Vince, who listened to these stories over and over again.

CHAPTER 1

Christmas, Present

The Driveway

There is the first ascent, then the angle in the bend is deep, and the road passes another house. Unlike me, people in that house have come and gone. I think the hardship of the road eventually obliges them to leave. After making the bend and passing that house, the driveway becomes long and steep. Overcoming the bend is an accomplishment that all regulars take pride in. They even tell of their personal battles and failures like soldiers tell war stories.

For 178 years, the dirt lane has defied repairmen, deliverers of goods, friends, and ultimately all who rely on it as the only way home. The battle has generally gone well for me. Starting up it, an act of faith is performed. It was at one time traveled, or travailed, only on foot or by animal and cart. Folks still find it forbidding even in an automobile.

I have walked it in joy, and it is beloved. I have walked it in trouble and even in despair. But in the end, it seems to me the most delightful highway of my acquaintance for after almost seventy years, it is as though it is my own substance dissolving in its ruts and runnels. It will be here long after I am gone. I think it is well to join ourselves to such things and be comforted.

The joining of person to place is a commitment to shared sorrow and to shared joy. This driveway (road, path) leads to a house. The farmhouse shabbiness is part of its endearing charm. When we have achieved restorations, they are good but somewhat at odds. Time eventually puts them right again. I prefer to reside in a state of genteel poverty, enforced by the cost of maintaining it than to surrender to mere comfort and some form of smaller, yet more respectable perfection in a newer home. When I am away from it, I feel a sense of homelessness. Then when I return, the mystic joy of childhood is regained.

Also, I need a certain remoteness from human confusion, and I take a backward pride in the barrier this road to home creates. Those who love me will continue to wrestle with it. And I am not offended when others are incapable of sharing or understanding its delights.

The consciousness of land must be deep within us. We cannot live without the earth, and something in us shrivels when we concern ourselves solely with the affairs of earning and buying. I am reminded of this daily when I come up the driveway. And so I remain cheerfully willing to do battle with it.

Christmas

Buffer was a tan collie. "Buff" colored. His name was one of Amy's mother's word games. She said he would buffer the two children from harm, buffer them from loneliness. This was how Ruth had wheedled her husband Bernie into getting the dog. "We live out here in the middle of nowhere, and they need someone to play with," she said.

So when Amy was five, Buffer had come into her life. And Ruth was right; he did keep her from being lonely. Bobby was twelve and loved the big dog, but when he went off to play ball and camp out and ride the horses, Buffer and Amy were together all the time.

The dog woke her up each morning with a nudge of the nose under her hand. This morning, she was in bed, half asleep, listening to the sound of her father shoveling the sidewalk. Buffer dug at her with his paw, and when Amy's eyes fluttered open, fifty years rocketed away to wherever decades and years and months go.

The light reflecting off the snow played on the cracked plaster of the high ceiling. The angle of winter light was the same as ever, but she realized as she awoke that it was 2009, and her husband Vince was outside clearing the walks. Her long gray hair spilled across the pillow as she turned over to look into the shining eyes of Spot, a twelve-year-old border collie who loved her in the same devoted way that Buffer had half a century ago.

This thing happened to her at times. Not quite dislodged in time, but often preoccupied by her nostalgia, she wondered if other people who had lived their whole lives in a family dwelling experienced their daily lives through a filter of collective memories.

She could look out of any window in the house, and as through a magic lens, she would see the time collapsing between the scene before her in the present, and the layers of events that had played out on this same land in the past. Where now a walnut tree stood, the shadow of a long-gone maple fell across the lawn in her mind. And then, many everyday objects would come under her hand, and a story would come into her mind unbidden. Even a smell could peel away years or decades.

Just now, it was time to get on with her day. It was Christmas, and she felt time pressing on her in many ways. She sat up in bed and made a list. There were pies to bake and most of the cooking to do, housework and a hundred other holiday tasks that she loved. A wave of childish excitement washed over her as she mentally collected great-grandma's tablecloth and the family tablewares she would parade out once again today. Spot followed her around as she made the bed and dressed. Just before she went downstairs, she paused for a long moment at the top of the stairs to remember…

The Tricycle Ride, 1961

The field had just been plowed. The little girl was sitting on the second floor landing at the top of the stairs, and she could smell the open earth. It was warm and damp after a spring rain, and the breeze rolled up the slanting field over the drive and picked up the aroma of early grass and dandelions as it rose through the sloping front yard. Like a wave, it came steadily up the concrete steps from the drive to the walk, up the steep front steps to the lacy Victorian porch, funneling in through the open front door and rising up the old wooden stairs to where she sat. Inhaling deeply, she could smell the worms, which were sunbathing on the wet sidewalk. She would have to include moving them all into the safety of the grass in her preparations.

She reviewed the plan. The hardest part was going to be getting the tricycle into the house and up the stairs. It was a heavy machine with fenders and a nice step in the back to stand on and push, which she did when she got it stuck in the mud or grass. She could pedal vigorously along the dirt driveway, but it was best when she rolled down the short front walk. There were only a few yards of pavement, and she wished there was a paved road she could ride on.

But back to the plan. The door would have to be propped open with something, like a rock or some books. The worms must be herded to safety.

The labor was intense. Amy was four and a half and small for her age but also strong and determined. Bringing the old red tricycle in the side door and through the living room, she then had to carry and drag it up one flight of steps. Her mother was hanging laundry out back, lilting phrases of familiar and made-up music. Sometimes, made-up silly lyrics were followed by a loud "cha cha cha" for no reason.

Hanging out the laundry was always a true rite of spring. It was exciting to have fresh sheets and towels the first time they were hung out to dry; the whole family was tired of basement-line-dried clothes smelling like the long winter.

The child was sweating by the time she got the tricycle positioned at the top of the stairs. She rested, perched on the bike, amazed at how much higher she felt compared to sitting on the top step there. Gazing down and out, she previewed her path: down the stairs, out the front door, across the wooden porch, down the flight of cement steps, down the short sidewalk, down the third set of steps, then across the dirt driveway and finally into the field below to come to a stop.

The front wheel inched forward. Just as it edged over the top step, she heard the back door open. Mum was singing at the top of her lungs. Amy had a brief flash of doubt, but it came too late. There was no way to stop now. Lurching forward, she almost went head-first, but she flung her weight back and jerked up on the handlebars. The rear tires were rolling down over the edge of the landing, and there was a deafening clanking sound as the tricycle hit each wooden step. Her feet were jammed onto the pedals, and the locked front wheel gave no relief to the increasing momentum. She was gaining speed steadily, and the front door rushed at her as though it was going to swallow her.

How quickly thoughts careen through our minds; as quickly as she was careening down the steps. Cool air rushed through her sweaty brown hair. She was still marveling at the tremendous echoing sound the stairs made as she rocketed out the door and across the front porch.

Her arms and legs were burning from the effort of clinging to her craft, and there was not even a split second to recover before she was going down the outside steps. They were concrete, and instead of the deep clunky clanking, she now heard gritty scraping of metal. She imagined that sparks were flying out behind her. Amy hit the sidewalk, and the front wheel snapped down forcefully. Her tiny white teeth closed with a furious click. Her mind registered the sound of Mum screaming somewhere high behind her. The startled woman was up on the porch, clean laundry trailing away in her wake, hands outstretched as though she could pull her child back with the magnetic force of a mother's desperation.

The smooth sidewalk that Amy had always loved now served her an extra helping of speed, and she realized with terror that it would not be possible to hold her weight back at this velocity, and she would probably go down the last set of steps head first. She closed her eyes at the last second and gripped the handlebars with all her might.

As she pushed against the pedals and locked her knees, her bottom left the seat, and her stomach turned over—she was airborne!

Opening her eyes and her lungs at the same time, she howled with glee, hurtling straight forward as if from a ski jump. For the rest of her life, she would have recurring dreams of flying, which were vivid and in which she relived the last few seconds of the tricycle ride.

All three wheels came down simultaneously. "Clump," said the tricycle. The earth was soft and damp and accepted the intrepid projectile and passenger warmly.

There was a joyous silence...well, silence filled with her mother's cries. "Oh...oh...oh!" Ruth couldn't manage anything more than single syllables. She was kneeling in the dirt beside Amy. "Are you all right?"

Smiling ear to ear, chin held high, Amy turned proudly to her mother. She was astonished to see that she wasn't delighted by the wonderful flight! She looked terrified; her face was white, and tears were spilling down her cheeks.

Brother Bob pulled the bike out of the mud. The wheels were buried. It made mucking sounds as he worked it out, and he was snickering and looking at her out of the corners of his eyes. She looked up at the house and saw just how far she had ridden—or ridden and flown.

After some days or weeks had gone by, her family began to enjoy telling people the story. She was mystified at the magic that time could weave. Because at first, she had been scolded and warned to "never, never do anything like that again." She had stood and watched as her father pried out and broke up the big concrete front steps and closed off the front porch railing to keep her or anyone else from tumbling down them. There had been frowns and warnings. She had been shown the chunks she had knocked out of the wooden stairs. And yet, now, at picnics or church, her mother, father, and brother had begun to relate the story of what she had done, with laughter and with all the wonder and pride that she had anticipated from the beginning.

Food Is Love

She descended, treading the worn and chipped steps barefoot. She let Spot out and became a whirlwind in the kitchen. She imagined an army of thousands of women all over the world, filled with Christmas spirit, doing the same.

The pumpkin for the pies was roasting in the oven. It was not one from her garden; it was from Shenot's Market. She had bought it in October, and it grew in prestige with each holiday. It had been promoted from lowly Halloween Porch Decoration to Thanksgiving Centerpiece to finally its lifetime ambition…Food! It was now at the very pinnacle of glory in this role, about to be part of one her famous Christmas pies. It smelled nutty and promising, a prophecy foretelling the wonders of a real homemade pie, one that would be tall, heavy, brown with molasses, and twice as much spice as the pale sweet empty pies from the bakery.

Amy was stubbornly proud about her pies and would not, could not roll out her crusts with any other implement than the huge maple pin with painted green handles. It had been her great-grandmother's pin, and Aunt Orie had given it to Amy when she left her home, Guffy Hollow, to come to The House.

At first, it had been difficult to wield so large a pin. It was made for a woman who had made twenty pies in a day, who fed boarders and coal miners and a family of bachelor brothers. Now that she had mastered it, Amy's hand rested coolly on the wood, which had rolled out hundreds of pies over almost as many years, and as she worked, she dreamed of the delight that her grown children would reward her with when they took the first bite.

Shenot's farm market is a last bastion of true Pennsylvania farming. Fifth generation farmers, siblings Diane and Ed Shenot and his wife Mary Lou have somehow managed to pass on to the next generation the love, the purpose of growing on the family land. The twenty-first century wells up around them, circles them like sharks. Throngs of businessmen and women come in large cars to buy the corn and tomatoes and homemade goods that stir something in them, a primordial sense of being connected to land and sky, which they themselves do not recognize or understand.

The customers crowd the market in October for apples, cider, straw, cornstalks, and pumpkins, not just to eat, but to use as decorations. They glorify the life which they crowd out with large plans of homes, schools, and traffic lights, where not so long ago, dirt roads crossed.

Alongside giant "jack-o'-lanterns," the Shenots still grow and sell "pie pumpkins," a designation needed only for the last few decades.

While the pies were baking, Amy decided to collect the preserves she needed. She went down steep cellar steps, and she smelled the earthen floor as she entered the basement room they called the fruit cellar. She picked up raspberry jam from the dusty oak shelf to put into her cranberry salad. She hoped that she also had ripe tomatoes for the other salad. As she had been taught, she had picked the last, best green tomatoes just before the first frost in the fall. They had been carefully inspected and wrapped in newspaper, then put in a basket on the cool basement floor. Over the winter months, many would rot, but about one half would ripen and present themselves on a winter table with the fragrance of midsummer. With a feeling of victory, she retrieved three nice ones. She returned to the warm kitchen and smiled as she flicked off the switch to the basement light.

The preserved raspberries were spectacular, and she was happy as she stirred them into the cranberry salad. The family loved raspberries, but not as much as they loved strawberries. Out back under the snow were a few hundred sleeping strawberry plants, a token reminder of the tens of thousands that once had populated almost every inch of the property. Amy and her brother Bob spoke often of their father's strawberry farm. They had planted, weeded, and picked beside him, and neither would ever taste a strawberry without comparing it to the ones that lived in their memories.

Bob had made a resolve that he would never spend a summer on his knees in a field again when he grew up. But for Amy, it was just the opposite. Growing berries with her father had planted the seed of garden love in her. Winter was a time for planning the garden, and when seed and nursery catalogs came in the mail each February, she would stick her head out the window and sniff for a whiff of earth. Drizzly spring days were spent in a Valhalla of mud and asparagus and onions. She was healed yearly by the salve of moist cool soil on her knees and hands.

Tomatoes and all sorts of berries hold first priority but are closely followed by radishes, lettuce, beans, and potatoes; grapes and fruit trees of all kinds proudly march in slow perennial step alongside the annual parade.

It was one of her life goals to imbue her children with an awareness of where life comes from, that we are not self-made; we are not an accident and we are not alone. A garden is where we all originally came from, and food represents so many aspects of respect for creation, love, self-sufficiency, and the ability to share and be hospitable. Growing food ultimately makes us humble in the face of forces we cannot control. The irony of our total dependence upon nature/creation, in order to strive for personal independence adds depth to our gratitude for a simple thing like a ripe tomato on the plate.

Phil in the Garden

Amy had entertained her children with made-up songs and parodies about gardening. The long summer days together in the sun were punctuated with songs and laughter, just as her childhood days had been. As she prepared to serve the holiday meal, she hummed one of her favorite parodies to herself.

Can Can

A parody to be sung to the tune of the "Can-Can" by Offenbach

Can can, this is called the Can can,
Cook it in a pan pan,
Put it in a jar, I don't know why it's called the
Can can,
Yes it's called the Can Can, Cook it in a pan and
put it in a jar, not in a can.

Tomatoes, squash and lots of kale,
The berries I picked in a pail;
Red ones, black ones also blue,
I'll make a jar of jam for you;

Then when all the jars are cool,
I will not rest I'm not a fool.
In the garden you will see
Ten thousand pounds of beans and me!

Can can, this is called the Can can,
Cook it in a pan pan,
Put it in a jar, I don't know why it's called the
Can can,
Yes this is the Can Can, Cook it in a pan and put
it in a jar, not in a can!

Christmas dinner was over, and all around the table, forks were being laid down one by one. From the seat that had been her mother's, Amy looked at the little family and was struck by the feeling of being part of what she called in her mind the "timeless march." Like Ebenezer Scrooge facing eternity, she "vowed that the past, present and future would strive together in her."

To her right sat Vince, in the spot her father had occupied. He smiled back with blue eyes filled with acceptance of this big emotion she was wearing, without knowing at all what it might be. Across from her was daughter Ruth, now twenty-six, in the seat that had been Amy's. Phil shared his side of the table with Uncle Bob, which was only fair; it had been Bob's all his life till he had surrendered it to Phil's high chair twenty-two years earlier. Bob had once shared that side with their grandfather. Curiously, the shift had moved the same direction as though time flowed counterclockwise around this little claw-foot table from Guffy.

Next to Vince was his mother, Beverly. She had drifted to the spot Aunt Orie had held to the end of her days in this house. Although Beverly was a polished, educated woman of business and society, and Orie had been raised in the Appalachian foothills and never finished grade school, they both had been forged into a certain character. Staunch, independent women who survived hardship. Amy was musing about these things and realized that Phil had spoken to her. He rose first from the table, as usual, and began to clear.

"Pie? Now?" he said playfully. He was tall and as slim as Bob had been at his age. Amy wanted to give him a whole pie right then and there.

"Sure!" she replied. There were groans of pretend anguish around the table at the thought of eating more; everyone agreed to wait for dessert till Vince finished doing the dinner dishes and Amy packed away the leftovers.

"Do you want to take some food home?" she asked, looking back and forth between Phil and Ruth and Bob. Three pairs of large brown eyes (all so much like her mother's that it tore at her heart) looked back at her. Phil and Ruth nodded yes eagerly, and Bob, as usual, said, "Nah, I'll come back and get some later."

On holidays, it was Bob's habit to sneak in late at night to raid the refrigerator. An event that has become a family joke, The Legend of the Pushpins, was invoked, and everyone laughed. Many years ago, Amy had spilled a box of pushpins on the floor near the refrigerator. In holiday fatigue and haste to get to bed, she did not pick them up. Howls of anguish arose from the kitchen around 2:00 a.m. Amy ran to the kitchen to find Bob, bare feet bristling with pins. This was a thing not to be forgotten!

As she tenderly bundled up the food for Ruth and Phil, Amy reflected on what such gestures mean. "Food is love," her children often teased. Today, it seemed that it might be true. Food is sacred; it is where nature meets culture, and after all, hadn't the Greatest One of all time used food to symbolize his giving?

From her earliest memory, Amy's parents had also used food to reach out to others. She looked at the tidy plastic containers in front of her, but in her mind, she saw a humbler version. She told the little group a story while they ate their pie.

Harriet, 1962

Snow burned Amy's ankles where it crept in between the tops of her black buckle boots and the legs of her snowsuit. As she trudged down across the front field, she hugged a warm basket in which nestled a Christmas dinner for two—turkey, stuffing, mashed potatoes, and an old peanut butter jar full of gravy. There was a tin can full of Dad's coleslaw, half a jar of cranberries, and two pieces of pie. At the bottom of the field, she skidded down over a snowy twenty-foot cliff on her bottom and slid to a stop at Harmony Road. After looking both ways and crossing the road, she trundled down the rest of the slope which was Harriet's yard.

Of all the houses she went to on Harmony Road, visits to Harriet's were by far the most unpleasant and the most alluring. Although Harriet was frightful to see, she laughed a lot. And her house was truly a place where even a child with no imagination at all could experience a different time and way of life.

She had once had red hair, which in itself was cause for fascination because it was now an unnatural pinkish gray. She had thick heavy glasses, and she was what people in those days called a "hunchback." Amy wondered why some frailties had titles like that and others didn't. You didn't call someone a "bucktooth" or a "fat bottom."

Treading upon her wooden porch, one expected the house to topple into a heap of weathered gray boards. On the other side of the tired Victorian door, the persistent odor of natural gas mingled with the smell of sickroom, Fels-Naptha soap, and kerosene.

Harriet kept everything. There were stacks of newspapers that went nearly to the ceiling, and five or six decades of church bulletins were amassed into towers. Strewn through the archives of post-cards and matchbooks were soiled rags and tissues and aluminum pie plates that looked suspiciously as though they had not been washed.

Ancient photos and documents made nests with green stamps, mouse traps, and receipts. Bandages swirled through porcelain tea-cups and spilled into heaps of greeting cards from this century and the one before. Nylon stockings and ancient flypaper dangled from the gaslights overhead.

The kitchen floor was as suspect as the porch and groaned when Amy squeezed her little body up next to the two-burner gas stove. This ancient appliance heated the house. Harriet was perched on a stool there in the corner, a tiny tin can of water coming to a boil for her tea. She was seated strategically so that she could see out the window up the hill toward Amy's house and also down the road. Nothing that occurred on Harmony Road escaped her eye.

In the room off the kitchen, Harriet's mother Katherine rested in a huge four-poster rope bed in which she had slept every night of her life since she had married Frank Frey in 1914. Harriet was an only child, born to them on April Fool's Day in 1920. Frank Frey said that she was such a homely disappointment that he was glad they had never had another.

She was redheaded, nearsighted and had a crooked spine and teeth. Frank never seemed to notice that she was bright, funny, hard-working, and as tough as nails. When he died, she got her first pair of spectacles and taught herself to read. She took in ironing and worked as milking girl on Klingensmith's farm, now Amy's home. The old gas well shack the two women lived in huddled below the front strawberry field. The Harmony Trolley Line, now Harmony Road, lay between Harriet's house, and the farm.

Katherine now was blind, deaf, toothless, and as thin as a piece of old linen. Harriet lived to care for her, and Katherine still enjoyed eating, and visits from "the little girl." No one ever knew how frightening it was for Amy to go up to her bedside and take the withered hand and try to make conversation as loudly as she could.

Amy knew no harm would come to her, and she felt good because she sensed that her presence gave the old woman happiness. But she could not understand why her mouth was dry, her heart beat faster, and she was so glad when she could leave. Every now and then, just out of the corner of her eyes, something would rustle in and out of the drifts of paper and old clothing that consumed the room. The only light was from a guttering kerosene lamp.

It would only be a few more years until Amy and her mother, Ruth, would stand beside the big old bed together, out of breath from running. "Mommy won't take her medicine," Harriet had wept over the phone. They had rushed down the hill through the field, entering the little shack without knocking. Ruth closed Katherine's eyes and told Harriet that her mommy was dead. Amy realized in that moment what it was she had been afraid of. But as it turned out, death was not so frightful; it was quiet and intimate and rather neighborly. She had patted the cool, dry hand and was not afraid.

Now on this Christmas Day, when Amy came into the house, there was a poinsettia perched atop the piles of newspapers beneath which a kitchen table surely lurked. Harriet opened the basket of food and inhaled. "Mommy and I sure will enjoy this!" Harriet asked Amy to sing a Christmas song for her and Mommy, so she sang "Silent Night."

"That was real nice, honey! You better get on back up the hill before it gets too dark," she said.

Amy looked over Harriet's crooked shoulder and out the window. Her own house was framed perfectly between the tattered curtains and the evening sky, which was still Advent-colored pink and purple. Yellow light poured down from the front porch like beams of light from the Christmas star.

"Okay. Merry Christmas, Harriet. I'll come back for the basket!"

Amy finished her story while the family savored the pie. The conversation resumed between bites.

"Did you go back for the basket?" Ruth asked.

"Of course. I visited all the old people on the road all the time. That is how I came to know much of the history of Warrendale and The House. Your grandfather always cut Harriet's grass for her, and after her well went dry, I carried water to her. I was still doing that when you guys were small. She told me stories about things like the night the barn here on our property burned down."

The Barn Fire, 1932

Klingensmith opened his eyes in the dark. On the ceiling were rectangles of flickering orange light, almost glowing. In an instant he was awake and realized that there was a fire. He heaved his meaty body out of bed and ran to the window. The barn was situated below the house and downwind. He couldn't smell the smoke, but he could see the flames and hear the animals—horses screaming and cows bellowing.

As he ran down the steps in his night shirt, he yelled for Harriet, the house girl, to wake up the farmhands. Without stopping for boots or coat, he was out the door and running through wet October grass, across the dirt driveway, and down the slope to the barn doors. It only took a minute to open the doors, and without hesitation, he was inside. Klingensmith worked his way blindly but surely from stall to stall, releasing the imprisoned beasts. One by one, they vanished into the thick smoke.

He wasn't a rich man, and he didn't have many animals. Two milk cows, a team of draft horses, and two ponies for the cart. And of course, his own horse. It had only been a few minutes, but he was struggling to breathe. Smoke ripped at his eyes and throat, and somehow, he found his way back to the big barn door he had come in. In a moment he was outside, and he saw his horses standing at the far end of the field, lit by moon and fire. Rows of corn stubble curved away past them into the darkness. Cold air washed against his sweaty face.

There was no water and no way to throw it, so he knew that his barn and everything in it were as good as gone. He felt a jab of pain in his chest as he turned to watch it burn. He looked up to the loft window. Silhouetted against the flames was his farm bell, of which he was so proud. It was a distinguishing feature of this farm. He wasn't sure who had put it there or when, but it was said that the Warrens had had it cast before the Civil War, and it had been calling cows home for eighty years since. When he rang it, everyone in the valley could hear it.

While he watched, he realized that his family was gathered around him, along with young Harriet and the two farmhands. He felt his chest tighten as he realized how many people this fire would bring hardship to. At least the livestock were safe. He took a deep breath and was about to ask the men to start to round them up and bring them in toward the house, but he couldn't speak. Searing pain brought him to his knees.

Klingensmith fell into the damp grass by a small mulberry tree. He looked up and saw a glistening red square, the frame around the bell, leaping with flames. As he drew his last breath, he saw William Warren's bell come clanging down through the sparks. He died just before it struck the ground.

* * * * *

The food was put away, the dishes were done, and her story was finished. Christmas dinner was over for another year, and Amy was happy to sit quietly as her little family moved around The House. After a while, they all packed up their presents and containers of left-overs, hugged and kissed Amy goodbye, and went out to their cars. It was quiet in The House. The wooden steps creaked as Vince crept up to bed, and she was alone. She went to the bay window, peered between the branches of the Christmas tree, and watched three sets of red taillights disappear down the steep driveway. She turned her attention to the tree. She fingered the decorations, some from her two great-grandmothers, some from her own mother, some made by her children.

She turned and went to the grand piano, sat down, and sighed. Then she slowly began to play. Every year, she played a tender Christmas song that her mother wrote for her in 1961. Amy loved it because it was naive and beautiful, because Ruth had sung it to her as a lullaby, and because it promised the joy of "hope in tomorrow" that is the heart and soul of Christmas.

"Tomorrow Is Christmas Day"
Ruth Stern

It's very late, the lights are low, come cuddle close to me,
Close your sleepy, dreamy eyes, and tell me if you see
Candy canes, Christmas lights, shining on the snow;
Silver tinsel, golden angels, candles all aglow.

Christmas cards, and jingle bells, ringing high and bright
Listen to the Christmas carols, echo through the night.

Taste the cookies, drink the wine, then you kneel and pray.
Time to go to sleep at last,
Tomorrow's Christmas day.

CHAPTER 2

The House

If you believe in love at first sight, you know it can happen between a person and a house. My mother fell in love with The House when she was a small child. It would be three decades until she saw it again. Many people fall in love with The House. They say that there is a sweet spirit, a peace, or a comfort when they come in. I wonder if it is the lingering fragrance of all the prayers uttered during the birthings and dyings that took place in the upper rooms; or maybe it is the living green serenity seen from every window on every side. Whatever it is, it called to her and to my father, and they found it.

Finding The House, 1958

"Ruth, I told the seller that as much as I want all twenty-five acres, I can only take five. I can't afford the down payment. I would need five hundred dollars more. But if they say they are willing to sell me the house with just five acres, I will take you to look at it. There is a great view of the valley facing toward the next town, Wexford. But I have to warn you. There isn't really a kitchen, it's just a pantry with a sink. But there is a big room we can turn into a kitchen. There are bats in the attic. No one has cut the grass for years."

"Are you sure five acres is enough, Bern? I mean for the horses and for the strawberries you want to plant?"

"Well, five is enough to pay taxes on," he replied and laughed.

"Take me to see it now," she said.

It was a quiet summer evening and they drove slowly from Evans City to Warrendale. Bernie drove and Ruth gazed out over the vast rolling fields and at the long low sunset.

Bernie really hoped she would like it. He felt as though it was meant for him. He had found a rundown place, but it was not expensive, and he could fix it up. "We will still be out here in the country where it is quiet and clean, but just not as far from work as in Evans City. We can afford this place. Nobody else wants a hundred-year-old house in the middle of nowhere."

As he turned off the highway into the dirt driveway, she said, "Holy Cow!" It was washed out with deep ruts, and water ran straight down the middle of it. They bounced and jolted around the bend, and by the time they reached the top of the hill, they were laughing.

When they reached the top, the sun was setting behind the empty house. In silhouette, it was tall with a slate roof and bronze and glass lightning rods. It needed a coat of paint, and the grass was knee deep. Bats were circling the old chimney in the gloaming. Bernie turned to look at Ruth. She was staring at the house, mouth hanging open, awestruck.

He thought she was horrified by the old place. She said, "How did you do this? How did you do this?"

He had no idea how to answer her. What did she mean?

"This is The House," she cried. "You know, *The* House!"

He knew if he said nothing and waited, the explanation would come tumbling out.

"This is The House that my grandfather and I passed on the trolley, the one I told you about! When we took the Harmony short line to Harmony for picnics! When I was little, I dreamed of having a house just like this someday. How did you find it?"

They bought The House the very next day.

The Move, 1958

Bobby and Amy sat in the "wayback" of the station wagon amongst rattling boxes and a few pillow cases full of laundry and the grocery sacks. It was the last load, the last trip. They looked out the back window and watched late September dust spiral away behind the old car as they rumbled along Evans City Road toward Warrendale. The tiny house they had just left disappeared from view.

"Take a good look, Ame," Bobby said. "We're never going back there again." The two-year-old started to whimper and looked around at her mother in the front seat.

"Oh, Bobby, quit it. Come on up here in my lap, sweetie." Ruth put the toddler in her lap. "We are going to our new big house on a hill." She comforted the tired little girl who nodded off to sleep.

When Amy woke up, she was still in her mother's lap, but the car was rocking and bouncing, and the others were all laughing. The car stopped in the dirt in front of a dilapidated two-stall garage with peeling green paint and a dirt floor.

They got out, and she held her mother's hand as they struggled through the weeds and then climbed slowly up some concrete steps. At the top of the steps, her mother paused. The sidewalk looked to Amy like a tunnel, with waving green grass towering over her head. Ruth looked up. They all did. There at the end of the grass tunnel was a flight of steps up to a pretty porch. Amy's eyes continued up, up to the roof of the tallest thing she had ever seen. The windows were dark and looked like an old woman's eyes. She looked weary but glad to see them.

1963

Rosie Mcpeak

Bernie was mowing the yards and parts of the fields that weren't plowed and planted with strawberries or corn. He loved his tractor. As he mowed, he thought about the day he had bought the 1948 International Harvester, in '59. He paid a little too much for it, but he loved it, and he needed it.

When he had tried to dicker with the old man who was selling it, the desperate old fellow had offered to throw in a mule. Now Bernie had no use for a mule, but he took a look just to be polite. His heart broke when he saw the pathetic lonely creature. It was bony and stood in a barren pen. There were few things that Bernie needed less than a starving old mule, but he felt pity for the animal and the man. He also really liked the tractor. Shaking his head more at his own folly than at what he saw, he said, "Okay, I'll take the tractor and the mule."

When he got it home, he tied it outside the pony shed and gave it water and some of the pony feed. He wondered what Ruth would say. She came out to the shed and first clutched the front of her housedress then ran over and hugged the mule around the neck. "Oh, oh, Bernie! The poor thing! Thank you!"

He looked at his wife. He loved her more every day. Ruth named the mule Rosie McPeak, after a song written during the depression about a black woman who visited prisoners on the chain gangs. Ruth made two ear holes in an old straw hat and put flowers on it and put it on Rosie.

Rosie was a nuisance. She kicked down every fence Bernie built; she pushed in the window screen and helped herself to food out of the kitchen sink. She never served a useful purpose other than as a conversation piece. She chased cars on the highway. But she lived out her last few years with people who cared for her.

He stopped daydreaming and looked up at The House. He had recently finished putting a fresh coat of paint on it. It was gleaming white. Bobby was out in front throwing a ball up into the air and catching it in his mitt. Amy walked behind the tractor and hopped on the lift bar behind his seat and hugged his neck. When they got to the bottom of the field, she jumped off and scampered away to look at something that caught her interest. The sun was hot, and the concord grapes were ripe and fragrant. Amy picked a bunch and ate them one by one. Perched on the cliff, she gazed down on the roof of Harriet's house. She decided to go down and ask her for a story.

The Summer Kitchen, 1845

"I was about ten years old when the summer kitchen at your place burnt down, around 1930 or so," Harriet said. "That was around the same time they got the electric in the main house. I never liked that electric. It's like lightning in your house. And me bein' a red head, we don't like lightning. It looks for us! He he he!"

Amy could never tell if she was serious when she said such things but she knew Harriet didn't like "the electric" because she refused to have it in her little home. The county tried to make her "improve her quality of life," but she stubbornly maintained that she had the right to live without electricity and running water.

Harriet was a good resource for stories about The House because she had always lived in its shadow. Today, she wanted to talk about the old summer kitchen.

"Ruth Warren and her hubby, who was a Fowler, built that kitchen in 1844, a year or so after they built The House. She was in the family way when they built, so they had to wait to finish it up. They had done a bang-up job building your house, I giss that's why it's still there."

She nodded her head and poked her chin in the direction of The House.

"Folks picked real careful where they built a house back then, for favorable livin', not just to be pretty like them in the seeburbs."

Amy tried to imagine Ruth Warren Fowler and her husband planning where the little outbuilding, so critical to the functioning of a home, would be. Harriet said they couldn't make it far away. Carrying hot food into the house from too far would be foolish. But if it was too close, the sparks from the chimney could land on the roof of the house.

The House is built on a breezy hill just below the crest. The chimneys drew very well. In fact, in every aspect the house is well situated. The front faces due east so light streams in the windows from the minute the sun rises and the back windows give light till the very moment before sunset. The well is only a few feet from the front door. Two terra-cotta French drains were put in behind and uphill of the house so the stone foundation stays dry even during heavy rain.

Harriet explained that the comfort and security of the house would be complete when the summer kitchen was finished. An additional bonus would be having the cooking implements and supplies out of the main living space and the big kettle and tripod out of the way. It would be a little more difficult to keep mice out of the goods but it was worth it.

In the end, the little outbuilding was built thirty feet from the back door on the north side of The House so that it would be cool in the morning. It faced east so that it had light very early. A wide stone fireplace was one whole wall, the north wall. Costly screen was installed on the two windows to keep flies to a minimum. There were wooden shelves and a heavy table, hooks for drying herbs and seeds. The earthen floor was moist the first year but soon became churned soft dust, which received drippings and small utensils silently.

The back wall had a wooden sliding panel about twenty-four inches square, about halfway up the wall. This window was the key to keeping the room clean. Scraps of food and vegetable peelings could be dropped out of it into a slop barrel that stood outside to be emptied into a pig trough every evening.

The window was also convenient for tossing out broken dishes, bottles—in fact, anything unwanted—into a heap just beyond the barrel. Anything that could be burned went in the fire, and rags and aprons went into a soak pot to be boiled on the fire after the cooking and dishes were done. It was efficient to run the clothesline from the summer kitchen to the house, and for most of the year, the cozy, tidy room doubled as a laundry and soap-making facility.

Cooking was not a periodic affair in those days as it is now. Food handling was a skill that included every aspect from dressing a fresh kill or catch, preservation of crops and orchard goods, to baking bread and making herbal cures and household products such as candles, soap, and liniments. Seed keeping was done in the house; the seeds were too precious to risk fire or rodents in the summer kitchen. Next year's life resides in the seeds.

The most important dimension was the distance from The House. If the kitchen burnt, it would not take the main dwelling with it. This distance also created a private domain for the woman of the house, where she could cry if she felt the need or steal a minute or two off her feet.

Harriet saved the most dramatic part of her historical recounting for last. "Ruth Warren must have spent some time cryin' in there. She had a little one named June, 'cause she was borned in June. But the whooping cough got her before she turned two." Harriet sniffled and wiped her teary eyes, genuinely moved by the sad story she told.

> My brother Bob and I had a path down through our front field. It joined Harmony Road, which we took to the school bus stop at Shenot Road. This path had been there before the road; Harriet said that the path was old, that in fact that it once was the road. It used to be called June's Gap,

named for the Warren's first child, who died as a toddler. It ran from our front door to the center of Bradford Woods, crossing Shenot Road where the old Harmony Short Line trolley trestle is today. Next to our field, it went through a tangle of crab apple trees that bloomed spectacularly each spring.

In 1997, I was leveling out a twenty-foot circle to receive an above-ground swimming pool, just off the north side of the house. Unintentionally, I became an archeologist. First I came upon spoons, bottles, and shards of broken dishes. I found one rectangular area very hard to dig and charred black, like baked clay, which I presume to be the site of the fireplace.

There were bricks scattered randomly and one rusted piece of a barrel hoop. In this story, I have reconstructed the summer kitchen from these finds, Harriett Frey's description of working there in the 1930s, and my own experience in the summer kitchen at the Fowler original homestead across the valley, which was still in use when I was a child.

Harriett believed that Ruth Warren Fowlers' summer kitchen burned down once in the nineteenth century and was rebuilt, burned again, and was finally demolished in the 1930s. A "modern" kitchen was added on the back porch of the main house; there was an icebox and a dry sink, and eventually electricity came to The House.

The Fruit Cellar, 1960

It was a love-hate relationship between the little girl and the fruit cellar. The thrill of anticipating the ruby red homemade strawberry jam she had been sent to retrieve was inextricably blended with the terror of going to the cellar alone.

Amy had watched last summer while her father ladled hot jam into the jars and carefully poured hot paraffin on the tops to seal them. She had watched him lovingly place the jars like shining soldiers in rows on the rough oak board shelf. She had played in the soft dust of the floor while he stacked his tools in the fruit cellar for the winter, next to the sleds, which she hoped would be brought out soon. The little room was cool. It was perfect for keeping potatoes, carrots, turnips, and beets.

Now, a dessert of bread, butter, and jam was promised on a winter's evening. She would have to overcome her reluctance to visit that room alone. The first hurdle was the steps. In daytime, she loved them. There was no problem because sunlight would be streaming in through the door at the bottom that let into a sunny room under the front porch. But in winter, right after dinner, it was like going down into a dark pit. Three steps from the bottom, just where the last of the yellow light tumbling down from the kitchen behind her ended, she was able to teeter up on her toes and grab the string that when pulled, turned on the single bulb in the ceiling off to the left.

The steps then cast a terrace of shadows to her right, across the fruit cellar door. It was painted glossy gray, perhaps seventy or eighty years before. The curling checks of paint made her think of her grandfather Puppo's alligator suitcase.

A bronze doorknob was the second hurdle. She unwillingly reached out to grasp his bulbous, flat brown nose, she hesitated as his tiny slitted screw-eyes scrutinized her. His keyhole mouth "oohed' a silent moan.

As soon as her little hand touched the cold metal, it became merely a doorknob again. But by now, her heart was pounding. The door swung inward, and as she knew it would, a wave of cool damp air carrying the scent of earth bathed her face. It was pitch-black inside; no light from the other room would turn the corner and enter with her.

The third and final hurdle lay between her and the prize. The string for the overhead bare light bulb in its ceramic fixture dangled in the darkness in the center of the stone room. Six feet of ancient earthen floor had to be traversed. She trotted forward, and then, standing in the dark, where she hoped it was, she waved her little arm feeling for the tattered string, eyes open wide, unseeing, unblinking, hoping for a clue as to where it hung.

In the instant when her hand encountered the string, a wave of heightened terror rushed through the little girl, who was sure that the sudden blaze of light would reveal some horror such as a skeleton, mice scurrying away from the food stored there, or something so much worse that she couldn't even imagine it in advance.

Click! The single bulb glowed warmly on rows of richly colored preserves. Tools leaned comfortably against the stone wall. Clean tan powder an inch deep squeezed softly up between her toes. White bars of paraffin (pronounced "pa-raf-feen" by her Aunt Orie) were stacked neatly on a piece of cheesecloth. One bar had notches made by the runners of Amy's and Bob's sleds, rubbed on to make them go faster. The enameled paraffin kettle stood at attention, waiting for active duty next summer when the berries would ripen again.

She selected a jar of jam, ran out, and scampered up the stairs with her mouth watering. She jumped into her seat, waiting for her mother to push the wax in with her knife and hand it to her to lick.

"Did you remember to turn off the light down there?" her father asked.

The Lost Keys, 1959

It was a time when children had simpler problems. But the problems were real, and many of these problems had to do with dealing with winter. Winter was more harsh and more personal. Neither clothing, nor vehicles, nor houses made winter so remote and polite as it seems today. People, even small people, spent time outside and had to deal with the elements. Toes and fingers could freeze inside rubber buckle boots and wet mittens. Colds could really kill you.

In spite of this, piles of deep snow, sleds, and toboggan trails carefully beaten down, frosted windows and frozen streams were all sources of fun and entertainment. Skating happened on ponds, not indoor rinks.

One deep cold winter Saturday, Bobby and Randy, who had spent the night, had a problem.

A lot of snow had fallen during the night. Bobby's father had driven toward Pittsburgh on McKnight Road to get the groceries early. Snow was still coming down. When he got home, there was so much snow on the steep driveway that even with tire chains on, Bernie could not get the car up the driveway. The two boys were put to the task of walking down to the car and carrying all the groceries back up the hill, about a quarter mile each way.

During the first trip down, they were warm and dry. They threw snowballs and laughed and pulled the lowest tree limbs down and shook the heavy snow onto each other. They stomped in the ditch to see if there was any water running under the ice.

The big station wagon was abandoned near the road at the bottom of the lane. Bobby importantly took off his mittens and fished the keys out of his coat pocket and unlocked the car. They stared at all the paper bags of groceries. They took two apiece, clutched them to their chests, and started the march up the hill.

Each successive trip to the car and back became less fun. They were getting sweaty, and their hands and feet were burning cold. Dad was on the tractor now, plowing the snow. The pristine white was piled as high as their chests on each side of the driveway. The scraped surface was slick.

On the fourth and final load, they had potatoes in a sack and sugar and flour—heavy loads. No laughing or snowballs now. Out of breath but victorious, they came into the warm house with the last of the supplies. Their cheeks were red, and Randy's glasses were steamed up. Wet mittens, boots, socks, snow pants with suspenders all were draped around on chairs and over the heaters. Puddles of melted snow turned the wax on the linoleum floor white.

"Let me have the keys, Bob," said Bernie. "Did you lock the car up?"

Bobby looked blankly at his dad. He had not locked the car.

"Well, find the keys for me. It's my only set. I will walk down and lock it for you."

The mountain of snow-soaked garb was ransacked, but no keys materialized. Bernie was worried. He glanced at Ruth. He only had the one set of keys. He had been meaning to get a spare made but somehow hadn't gotten around to it. Without the keys, he would never get to church tomorrow—or even worse, to work on Monday.

Bobby piped up, "I'll just go out and find them, Dad!" He grinned his "please-believe-me-and-don't-be-mad" grin. "First thing in the morning, me and Randy will!"

"Randy and I," Ruth corrected.

"Yeah! Him and me!" Bobby reiterated. Bernie just sighed.

The boys were up very early Sunday morning. At breakfast, Bobby asked, "Dad, where is the brace and bit?"

"What for?"

"I need to make holes in the snowbanks where you plowed, so I can look into the snow for the keys," Bob explained.

Randy nodded. They looked earnestly at Bernie. He fetched the brace and a big auger bit as well as his camera. Ruth looked at him over her glasses questioningly.

"I'm going to take a picture of this process," said Bernie.

"Yeah, a picture of me and Randy finding the keys!"

The Lost Keys

All the snow clothes were dry, and as soon as the boys went outside, they bolted down the driveway about fifty yards and slid to a stop. Bernie trudged up to them and was setting the speed and F-stop on the little brownie camera as Bobby instructed Randy where to drill into the hard-packed snow. Then he bent over and peered into the one-inch hole. "Take a look. There they are, Randy," he crowed.

"How do we dig them out, Bobby?" (Randy viewed Bobby as the brains in this operation.)

"Let me see," Bernie said incredulously. He bent over and peered into the hole. "Well I'll be damned." He had expected this to be one of Bob's jokes, but there they were. One guess, one hole, one set of keys. He took the boys' victory picture and always swore that the story was true.

They weren't even late for church.

Time Drifts

Time behaves like water—gently flowing at times, a rushing torrent at others. When we are very busy or preoccupied, it seeps away. When we are wasting it, it evaporates. Once time flows into the past, it freezes solid, into immovable glittering sculptures or hard stinging drops.

Sometimes, it freezes into small dry flakes, at other times into lazy big wet flakes that blow into great drifts. These drifts pile up, not in alleys or corners but in places that take us by surprise. I always anticipate a time drift in places like museums, antique stores, or pawnshops.

I have stumbled and fallen into a very deep time drift in places that take me off guard, such as my old grade school. Once, I was almost buried alive in a time drift in a waiting room when a song came on the radio that my mother used to sing to me.

I live in a house that traps time. Because of this it is very important to make sure that I spend a lot of my life in the present. But the present has a knack for becoming the past at an alarming rate.

The Young Carpenter, 1905—the Indian Trail and the Bay Window

Clyde Uhlenburg was quiet as he walked quickly up the driveway, carrying his tools and his lunch. His heart was singing. Early morning sun slanted from the valley on the east and glistened on the may-apples that lined the northern uphill side of the rutted dirt lane. Behind the may-apples, a colonnade of tall pine trees roughly followed the Kuskusky Indian trail, parallel to the driveway.

Today was a red-letter day. After working just one year for Mr. Fowler, who owned the lumber company, he was to have a chance to do a project by himself, from start to finish, of his own design. If it was good enough, he was to be advanced to finish carpenter.

They were repairing the rundown old Warren/Fowler farmhouse, where his buddy Chester Fowler was born. The work had to be done to last another lifetime. *Do all things as unto the Lord*, he thought.

The plans were in his pocket, but they were also in his head. Perhaps they would think it too fancy for the old house. They might laugh. He might be chastised for taking too long, but how else could he show them what he could do? It was a risk he had to take. He had been given good oak boards.

The original wide plank pine floor had been walked out. He was to make a new floor, and not just for the original room but also for the new bay window and the little vestibule at the front door. A big bay window for light was being added on the north side, and a fine porch was being built onto the front.

Until now, there had been only a simple narrow wooden staircase up to the high front door, a common inconvenience of houses built on Pennsylvania hillsides in the nineteenth century. The new porch would have a roof, decorative railings, and wide cement steps going down to a sidewalk, if you could imagine that. A farmhouse with a sidewalk. Well, he thought, it is a new century.

At any rate, there was to be an oak floor when you came in the door but very tiny, as the steps to the second floor were right there. How could he make this beautiful and yet make sense when it flowed immediately into two rooms, one on each side, with steps in the middle?

His floor would solve all the problems and be beautiful. It would unify all the little spaces. He had a spiral of boards in his mind's eye, starting in the middle of the front room, simply beginning with a small rectangle of boards that continuously ran around itself until long fifteen- to eighteen-foot sections swept the baseboard on every side of the room. The bay window floor and the little vestibule would be the same pattern in miniature. A fine design indeed, a bit fancy for the home but lovely to make and see.

He would make every tongue and groove tight and every corner square, except where he had done the best design work of all; he would make many tiny adjustments as he went along so that by the time the spiral hit the walls, they would conform to the no-longer-square room. He would disappear the effects of time. His boss would be impressed.

When Clyde arrived, he set his tools down and saw that his boards were piled neatly in front of the house waiting. He took a minute to look out over the valley as the sun rose higher. Clyde smiled. He wondered if fifty or one hundred years in the future, someone would marvel at such a fine and fancy floor in such a plain old farmhouse.

> When Clyde was eighty-seven, he told this story to me as I sat on his lap in his home at 105 Harmony Road, near the bottom of our driveway. He had become a finish carpenter in 1905 after making that floor and in his lifetime worked in many fine homes, but that floor was the one he loved the most. He taught the design to a fellow named Ben Whiteside in about 1935, who built a home for himself at 107 Harmony Road. Ben was about ninety-five when I saw him last in 2005.
>
> Chester Fowler would build Fowler's Motel on a piece of the Fowler homestead across the valley from me, just across Route 19 from the

Fowler Homestead house. There are car dealerships there now. I witnessed the homestead house burn to the ground when I was twenty-one years old. I also knew Chester's father, who was Clyde's employer in the story, William "Grandpa" Fowler. He died at the age of 102 in 1966.

The floor pattern survives in my home and in the red brick house on Harmony Road.

Clyde told me the history of the Kuskusky Indian Trail, which parallels the driveway to this day. He said to me that in the 1880s, when he was little, travelers on foot still used it to come through Warrendale. He said it roughly ran north to south across Marshall Township where old Route 19 is and eventually joined the Venango Trail. (Judith Oliver documents a detailed history of this trail in The History of Marshall Township).

The trail runs north to south behind The House and then turns due west, goes along, and then crosses Vander Road in the section where Hermit's Rest used to be. Thousands of bare and moccasined feet trod this trail. It is a pleasant invitation to the woods, and it was a highway. It was a strong footpath when we were children. By the time that this portion of it came to be mine, it was still evident to the careful eye.

As of today, it is perhaps the last unpaved and wild portion of the original Indian highway. Each time I visit the woods, it has faded more from disuse, but I still can follow it. I believe I am the last living human creature who can do so.

Just beyond the edge of my domain, it turns south again and crosses Wheatland Road and is the main entrance to Wheatland Point. After the cul-de-sac, it ends at the section that was in

Shenot's Orchard Valley. I witnessed that portion being bulldozed in 1974 for the construction of Interstate Highway 79.

They're Here. They're Here! 1962

Bob yelled, "They're here! They're here!" and Amy ran to the bay window to catch the first glimpse of the most exciting thing in the world, which was company! No one was in the driveway and Bob snickered. It was the third time that day she had fallen for it.

Eventually, the company did arrive, and he called out the ritual signal. When she looked out the window, she was rewarded by the sight of Aunt May, burdened with a casserole dish, a board game, and a bag, which surely held wonderful small homemade gifts. Uncle Bert was stretching and feasting his eyes on the front field and the view of the valley. Cousins were pouring out of the back of the station wagon.

Just then, another car pulled up. It was the Thomases. Friends of Mum and Dad, they brought such wonderful things as cheese curls, macaroni salad, Kool-Aid, and billows of cigarette smoke to add to the parental cloud suspended above the card tables. They also brought two teenagers who lurked around reluctantly but were still interesting because they were different.

It was Labor Day. The swimming pool was warm, tomatoes were still on the vines, and corn was full in the ear. Everyone settled down around the picnic tables, which were actually huge wooden cable spools that the telephone company had discarded. They looked just like giant thread spools, and Bernie had painted them orange, red, yellow, and green. They were easy to move; you just rolled them around and plopped them into place. Hot dogs and hamburgers had been eaten, and the charcoal grills still gave out the hot signature smell of picnic.

After one hour of waiting "so you don't get a cramp and drown," the above-ground swimming pool was reopened. The children swam so long that their fingers were wrinkled and their lips were blue. All of a sudden, there was a great splash! Bernie canonballed right into the center of the round pool. The kids all dove on him and hung on his neck. It was a group effort to pull him under, but even with five or six children hanging on his neck, he roared and swung around and flung them off like a bucking bronco.

When they tired of that, he initiated the "whirlpool." Everyone ran around the perimeter of the pool in one direction until he yelled, "Reverse!" Children of all sizes fought the current and were swept around till tired out.

Just when it seemed like time to get out, Bernie reached over the edge of the pool with his long arm and produced a lit cigarette from Ruth's ash tray on the picnic table. He filled his lungs with smoke and disappeared under the water. Teeth chattering, the children stood still and waited—smoke bubbles exploded to the surface all around them. They shrieked and chased the smoke as it vanished.

He burst up out of the water and yelled, "Everybody out of the pool!" Wet, shivering children wrapped up in thin damp towels and stood around, wondering what there was to eat. The towels were not big beach towels. They were the oldest most worn towels a household could produce, just one step before the rag bin. They had been used over and over again all day until it was likely that they got the little swimmers more wet than dry.

"Ruth, put some water on to boil," he said. "These kids are going to pick corn."

The sun was setting, but the evening was still warm. In the dusk, the corn patch looked vast, wild, and tall to the children. Lightning bugs were just starting to pop in the cornrows. The damp towels all hit the ground as the wet children ran barefoot toward the field.

Long scratchy corn leaves dragged along their damp limbs. They felt in the near-dark for the fattest ears and pulled them from the stalks. Amy paused for a moment and stared straight up past the tops of the tasseled plants, hugging her ears of corn to her chest. The stars were coming out, and the sky still looked light compared to the darkness deepening around her in the corn.

One by one, children emerged from the field with their little harvests and ran toward The House. They sat together on the front porch step and husked the corn as fast as possible, leaving the pile of husks on the sidewalk. Corn silk clung their ankles and feet. While they worked, the windows became squares of yellow light. Inside, the women had put large pots of water on every burner and slabs of golden butter on plates. The adults sat at the table, and children stood around or sat on laps. They reached past parents, aunts, and uncles to roll the steaming hot corn in butter. Butter ran down to their elbows.

As they devoured the fresh corn, Uncle Bert said, "Hey, Bern, there's a worm in my corn. Why don't you spray it?"

Bernie stopped eating and looked at him kind of puzzled. "Who wants to eat something that kills everything that eats it?"

Cob technique was discussed. Ruth proclaimed that the best way to eat corn was left to right like a typewriter. Bobby proudly announced that his cobs came out square! Amy was struggling to clean her cobs because she was missing two front teeth. Little cousin Joanne just licked salt and butter from hers and then rolled it in butter again.

Eventually, everyone was full. The men stood out in the yard and smoked while mothers put children in pajamas and herded them to the cars. Ruth wrapped her arms around Amy, and they stood in the bay window and watched as red taillights disappeared down the driveway.

Then the night was quiet and dark.

CHAPTER 3

The Town

Greetings from WARRENDALE, Pennsylvania

It is comforting to live in a community for so long that you knew the people for whom the roads were named. Shenot, Cole, Logan, Warren, Frey, Neely, Fowler, Slade, Enders—the list goes on. Eventually, when I and a few others are gone, many of those folks will be forgotten, and only the names will remain.

I am glad the roads are so named. They remind us that people were here before roads and buildings and that those people stood on ground that they had to clear, till, and build on; that they contributed in church and town; and were needed and loved. They worked hard and made a mark.

Why do we love to talk about the past? Because our stories tether us to reality. When we tell the stories, we link hardship to reward, discipline to success, and effort to character. So we name roads and parks for the people who came before in the hope that we will remember their stories.

Mashey's Farm, 1961

Bernie was jingling his keys in his pocket. "Who wants to go for a ride?"

The question was directed at Amy, who never turned down an opportunity to go somewhere with him.

"Where are we goin', Dad?"

He loved the look of anticipation in her eyes.

"To Mashey's to get the milk. Grab the cans."

There were two galvanized aluminum milk cans outside by the faucet, freshly washed and ready to go. She struggled to push the tight-fitting lids on and followed Bernie to the truck. She rolled the window all the way down and let the summer evening breeze blow-dry her sweaty face and hair. The road was so bumpy that she bounced around on the seat of the truck, and the milk cans clanked around at her feet.

Bernie drove slowly down the lane, letting his daughter savor the sights and smells of the dairy farm. Looming ahead was a long creamy white barn, which appeared to have made its home in the only level space. It sat in a cheery hollow between two smooth-looking airy-green fenced-in pastures, which were the same color as lacewings or praying mantises.

As they pulled in, dusk was falling, and the march of the cows had begun. In slow motion, the sweet animals fell into formations and moved gracefully toward the gates in the respective fences, one on the left and one on the right of the barn. Lightning bugs twinkled trustingly under and around the giant creatures.

Mr. Mashey opened one gate, then the other. He stood still in the current of cows, which flowed past him closely, and he calmly patted one or another of them; he muttered kind words to them.

Slowly he followed the last one to the barn. Just next to the door was a well with a hand pump. It was equipped with a bar of Fels-Naptha soap and a square stone basin beneath it that was large enough that a man could stand in it and wash his boots. It was imperative to be clean before entering the dairy.

Mr. Mashey looked at Amy. "If you want to go in the dairy and talk to the girls, you know what to do."

She was very familiar with the routine, so she stepped into the cement trough and scrubbed her hands and arms up to the elbows and then her little bare feet with the rough soap. Bernie and the farmer talked about all the same things they always did—tractors, how tall the corn was, when it would rain, what the president was doing. Amy was now rinsing off, so Mr. Mashey nodded and tipped his head over toward the barn door without interrupting Bernie.

As she stepped into the warm barn, the thick quiet of hay and cows swallowed her, and the men's voices faded away. She could hear only the shuffling of giant feet on straw and the creaking of the old structure and an occasional conspiratorial moo of one cow to another.

A few turned their heads slowly and looked through long lashes at the little girl. So Amy petted, stroked, and hugged cows and calves, telling them all about her little girl world. It grew dark outside and buttery yellow light streamed out of the barn.

She knew that it was time to go when Mashey came in and milked for them. It took just a few minutes to fill their two cans. Bernie gave him a dollar and shook his hand.

Back in the truck, Amy wore a perfume of cow, hay, and soap. When they got home, Bernie poured the milk into glass gallon jars, which went into the refrigerator, and Amy went up to take her bath. She couldn't wait to get back down to the kitchen. Her mother was ladling the cream off the top of the cooled milk into pint jars. She handed one to Amy and two to her husband and took one to her rocker by the window. Father and daughter grinned at each other and started to shake the jars. They shook and shook and shook them, and when her arms grew tired and started to burn, Amy got out of her chair and danced around with her jar of cream. They were laughing now, and Bernie kept a steady rhythm.

"Let's check now, Dad," Amy cried.

"Not yet. Keep shaking!"

Her arms were aching and burning. Just when she was sure she couldn't do it anymore, Dad said, "Let's take a look."

He unscrewed the cap and let her peer in. Little pea-sized lumps floated in the milk—butter! The lid went back on. He handed it back to her, and they both started to shake their jars again. "Better get the crackers out, Ruth. It's almost done."

Finally, they were sure it was ready. This time, when Bernie took the lids off, there were butter balls bigger than lima beans. The milk was strained off into a glass for Amy, and the butter was packed into a blue and white bowl.

When Bobby came in the door from his ball game, it was ten o'clock. "Oh boy! Butter and crackers!" They sat around the kitchen table and spread the soft fragrant butter onto saltines and talked and laughed.

Amy was tucked into bed and fell asleep listening to tree frogs and thinking about cows.

The Strawberry Stand, 1964

A car in the northbound lane of Route 19 slowed down, hesitated as though it could not make up its mind, then continued on its way. Amy knew it would go about half a mile to the next intersection, make a U-turn, and come back to where she waited on the southbound side of the highway.

It happened a lot; in fact, most of the first-time customers were northbound and could see the eight-foot-tall sheet of plywood that was the sign for the fruit stand. Southbound drivers passed by, never knowing what they had missed.

Amy's father had painted the sign. It was a huge strawberry. The detail was marvelous. There were seeds (which were as large as Amy's hand) and green leaves with shiny spots, all seeming almost three-dimensional, they were so detailed and faithfully rendered. Simply, boldly, the sign proclaimed 50 cents!

It was not really a fruit stand. It was actually an assortment of folding tables and a picnic table covered with gleaming quarts of strawberries picked less than an hour ago, a wooden box for money, a little stool, and a red plaid thermos full of cold water.

The big car wallowed to a stop in the grass at the side of the road. A large man in a suit and a small woman in a flowered dress emerged. She had painted fingernails and big earrings. "Oh, do you grow these beautiful berries yourself, sweetie?" She was smiling and digging in her large shiny purse for change while she talked.

Amy smiled back. "My dad does, and my brother and I help." The woman bought five quarts. "That will be two dollars and fifty cents, please."

She gave the little girl three dollars and said, "Keep the change for yourself, honey."

It had taken several trips down the driveway and back up to the field to get set up that morning. The tables and equipment had been the first load. Then, Dad had filled the whole back of the station wagon with quart baskets of berries on a sheet of plywood, which he and Bobby slid out so she could unload them onto the tables.

Before they left to go get the next load, Bernie squatted down in front of her. "Let's see what you look like." He smiled at her. She was small for a seven-year-old, had freckles and crooked teeth. Her bare feet were dirty. He took a ripe berry and took a bite. Then he dabbed the berry on her chin and the tip of her nose. "You look perfect," he laughed. "You'll sell out!"

They had picked about eighty quarts that morning, and by noon, they were sold. Bernie and Bob picked berries all afternoon while Amy played. After dinner, the tired father let his son go free and loaded the station wagon with another load of berries.

"Can I go down to the road with you, Daddy?"

"Sure, if you want to." He was pleased.

She sat on the tailgate of the car in the shade and watched him sit by the tables. There were long, quiet stretches of time between cars and longer stretches between customers. He sat very still with his long legs crossed. He looked very relaxed. He was sunburned, and his blond hair was wind tousled. He had a handkerchief tied around his neck.

Every car that pulled in produced a cheerful customer. They all exclaimed at the exceptional quality of the berries. Each box was heaped as full as possible. He had taught the children to put only fully ripe berries with no bad spots into the baskets. She observed closely the pride her father took in providing the best product he could and how much he enjoyed the friendly, comfortable exchanges with the customers. He shook the hands of the men after they paid, and if a woman offered her hand to shake, he dusted his hand first on his pants before he took it.

Soon, it was getting dark and there were just a few quarts of berries left. They gathered them and the box of money, leaving the tables for tomorrow. Amy was happy as they rode up the hill. She sat on the open tailgate and watched the dusty driveway roll away under her dangling feet.

The smell of the berries blended with that special cool smell that comes out of the woods at sunset. Fireflies sparkled low over the fields of berry plants. She knew that her mother would slice up what hadn't sold and mix them with sugar. They would sit in the kitchen and eat as many as they wanted with ice cream or milk or just ripe brilliant red fruit by the bowlful.

When they couldn't eat any more, the rest of the day's pick went into a pan for jam. While it simmered, Ruth leaned against the stove and watched her husband count the money. Even though he had scrubbed his hands, they were stained from picking thousands of berries. It was a ritual for him to make a report. First, he announced the day's sales, in quarts and in dollars, then the total for that season to date and a projection of what they would sell the next day.

Tired, full, and happy, Amy crawled into bed. When she closed her eyes, she could see strawberry leaves and fruit on the inside of her eyelids. Voices from the kitchen drifted up the stairs with the smell of jam.

Book Club Christmas, 1964

During the long summer, Amy had read every age-appropriate book in the bookmobile and several for older readers. The small trailer full of books circulated weekly to towns with no public library. When school started each fall, she always looked forward to the arrival in the classroom of the monthly catalog of the Scholastic Reader's Book Club. This was exciting but bittersweet. There were so many books from which to choose, but she was given a modest budget and had to be very selective. Unlike many of the other children, she did not waste her allotted spending power on rubber erasers, bookmarks, pens, lapel pins, book covers, or any other paraphernalia that indicated that one was a member of the reader's club. It all went for books. She wondered if the other kids had more money or less interest in reading than she.

The price of the books ranged from seventy-five cents to four dollars. Ordinarily, she had three dollars each month. So if she chose all paperbacks, she could get a few nice selections. After agonizing over the catalog, she carefully filled out her order blank and put the correct amount in the envelope with it and walked forward and laid it on Mrs. Johnson's desk on December 10. The teacher smiled and said that the books would come in about two weeks.

This month was very different when it came to book club. She had been given the extraordinary amount of ten dollars for books as part of her Christmas present. She would have twelve days off school and time to read, read, read! Christmas vacation started on December 23. What if the Scholastic Reader's Club book order didn't come in time? She had ordered some wonderful books, such as *Eighth Moon* by Bao Sansan as told to Bette Lord, *The Shaman's Last Raid*, *Little Women*, *Old Yeller*, *The Adventures of Huck Finn, and The Adventures of Tom Sawyer*, and most ambitious of all was a biography of Abraham Lincoln. She would just have to wait. Asking Mrs. Johnson everyday if the books had arrived didn't make any difference, but somehow sharing her sense of urgency with the kind teacher eased the stress.

On the last day of school, the book orders did in fact arrive. Mrs. Johnson said that the book orders would be distributed at the end of the day. Morning was the in-school Christmas choral concert followed by lunch. The afternoon had been spent cleaning out the cloak room. Each child emptied his cubby, bench space, and cloak hook, and then went through the lost-and-found bin to claim gloves, hats, hair berets, and yo-yos.

The fourth graders swept and scrubbed the little room as a group, with much crowding and laughter, fueled by candy-cane-induced holiday hysteria. Each one had a large paper sack full of papers and clothing and also book orders to carry home. The final bell rang, and all six classrooms of children poured from the building. It had been snowing all day, and outside, it was perfectly deep white and blue, holy-looking winter.

When she got off the bus, Amy had a lot to carry. Harmony Road had been plowed, so it was easy going until she reached the point where she left the road to take the path through the field. Climbing first over the bank of plowed snow, she dragged her paper sack after her. The snow in the front field was about two feet deep. She was wading and falling, laughing and sweating. As she clambered up the final slope to The House, she could hear Christmas music playing and her mother singing at the top of her lungs. The Christmas tree was lit and glowing in the steamy bay window.

Amy never knew what would be going on in the kitchen when she got home. Today, the kitchen door opened on a fantastic scene accompanied by the smells of vanilla and peppermint and blaring Christmas music. It was not unusual to be greeted by the smell of donuts, or turpentine, depending on whether Mum was hungry or seized by the desire to oil paint. Today, the kitchen table was littered with branches, dead tree branches spread out on newspaper surrounded by pots of candy! Next to the stove was the ironing board, draped with wax paper and covered in pastel rows of candy. Yellow lemon fondant balls and pink and green peppermint patties. Mum was beaming and singing and dancing around the branches with a large paint brush and a pan full of sugar candy glaze. She was engrossed in draping ice-clear candy icicles on the branches, which were already covered in convincing white fondant candy snow!

"Wow!" Amy yelled. "What are you doing?"

"Well, I was watching it snow while I made Christmas candy, and I started thinking that the trees looked so delicious, I wished you could eat them. So I decided to go get some branches and make candy branches! What d'ya think, kidface?"

She was obviously high on sugar and music and fun.

"Where are we going to put them?" asked the enchanted child.

Ruth was stumped for a minute. *Put them?* she thought. *Oh! Right!* Dim thoughts of needing the kitchen table for dinner time and Bernie coming home from work began to percolate.

"Let's put them all over the house! On top of picture frames, on the piano and the organ, and bookshelves! It will be winter indoors! And anytime you want some candy, you just take it!"

While Amy decorated the house with candy branches, Ruth started to fry some onions in butter. She believed that being greeted by this wonderful aroma gave her husband hope when he came in the door from work tired and hungry. She packed up the candy from the ironing board, making up one spectacular plate and putting it in the center of the now clean kitchen table, adorned by a tiny white candy branch. The package of new books was waiting front and center under the Christmas tree, right in front of the manger scene.

When Bernie came home, the aroma of dinner greeted him. He found his son playing records, his wife making dinner, and his daughter on her belly in front of the tree. Her feet were in the air, and her nose was in a book. He stood there for a moment just taking it all in and trying to figure out how and why there were branches all around the house covered with snow and ice.

The Bell, 1965

The large bell lying beside the driveway was sunk far enough into the dirt that it could not be rung. If you hit it with a stick it merely emitted a dull thud. Tufts of tall seedy grass grew up around its rim. Sometimes, when she was playing near it, Amy would run her hand over it and wonder why it was there. She scampered past it every day. It was a fixture, just like a tree or a fencepost.

But now, the bell was leaving. Missionaries had come to The House; Father Dougherty had asked if someone from the church could put them up while they were visiting, trying to raise money for their mission in the Philippines. Housing them was a special privilege. The two men stayed in Amy's room, and she slept in Bobby's room.

On Sunday, after Mass, Mum had prepared a company meal. There was roast beef with her wonderful gravy and mashed potatoes and bowls of fresh sliced strawberries from the top field. Over dinner, conversation had turned to the bell resting in front of the house.

The older of the two men spoke very softly. "We have no bell for our little church, Mr. Stern. In front of your house, I see a bell that seems not to be in use."

Bernie explained that the bell had been sleeping there since a long-ago barn fire brought it to the ground.

"Your bell can have a new life, Mr. Stern."

Bernie imagined the bell, transformed from forgotten farm bell to missionary bell serving God. After only a few minutes, it was decided that the bell would be sent to the mission.

Exhuming the bell was a solemn and important ceremony. Bernie pried it gently up out of the ground, and Amy helped him to clean the caked mud from it. They rubbed it with oil. He built a wooden crate around the bell, and men from the church helped him to load the old bell onto the pick-up truck. Oliver the postmaster weighed it, and it disappeared into the back room of the post office. Amy had a sense of loss.

Sitting on her mother's lap, Amy peered at the tiny little green dots in the blue ocean part of the globe. Ruth explained that these were islands that people lived on. Amy imagined tiny churches and tiny houses on the tiny island dots. "Our bell will be in a church in the Philippines, halfway around the world. It has been resurrected!" She said that it would be rung when something good happened, like when Mass was starting, or when someone got married. They would ring the bell when someone died or there was an emergency. She said that when they had a school, they would ring the bell for that as well. Amy could see that giving the bell away made her parents happy, so she decided to be happy too.

The Tin Cup, 1963

Everyone who grew up Catholic in Warrendale and Wexford remembers the smell of the church. Although they did not know it,

Saint Alphonsus Church greeted those who entered with the same smell as the great old cathedrals of France; a blend of damp cold stone, incense, burnt beeswax candles, flowers, sweat, and wet woolen coats. These smells were layered together year after year. There was no ventilation in summer, and in winter, no central heating.

During Mass on snowy days, gray drips of melting slush dripped from boots and shoes and made pools under the pews. The dampness lingered through the arrival of balmy spring Sundays. On a soft rainy Easter, the enormous wooden doors were flung open allowing a breeze of hyacinth to bathe the faithful. The dampness persisted into muggy summer days. Then the humidity rose so high that even though it felt cooler inside than the steamy August morning outside, worshippers would be sweating before reaching the pew. The holy water into which they dipped their fingers to make the sign of the cross was warm, and the drops on their foreheads did not evaporate.

Within a few minutes, the music from the organ eased the transition from the regular world outside into this world of high, damp space. No one spoke; heads were bowed in prayer, or eyes were trained on large sculptures of the saints, tinted and mellowed with soot and dust, which made them seem a thousand years old and very sacred. Someone coughed but only quietly, and it blended into the soft shuffling of feet as people kneeled and prayed. You could hear a page turn as someone prayed from their Saint Joseph Missal. From some hands, rosaries dangled over the pews.

Mass was Latin, high, beautiful, and long; little girls' bare knees stuck to the film of grit on the kneelers. Very old people would eventually tire and either half kneel by leaning back against the pew, or they would even sit but only if they were very old. All women and girls wore fashion-mandated white gloves and church-mandated head coverings—a hat or a lace mantilla, which trapped heat and perspiration. Men and boys wore suits and ties and carried handkerchiefs with which they mopped their faces and necks. The celebrant was in full robes, each garment heavy with meaning and tradition. There was no water fountain.

When mass ended, the pipe organ pealed a processional and everyone felt elated. Since there was a fasting rule before mass, lunch was much anticipated, but not as much as fresh air. Everyone flowed outdoors in one smooth exodus, breaking into cheerful greetings as soon as they descended the stone steps and reached a respectful distance from the doors. One little girl turned and wriggled out of the column of bodies just before exiting. She turned left and squeezed into the little winding wooden staircase that went up to the organ loft, feeling the wall in the dark and hurrying to get all the way up and hover next to Betty, the organist, before she finished the recessional.

Betty was enormous and ancient and seemed to be part of the huge old instrument. Summer and winter, she wore a long gray sweater, which draped over the high bench. Her stockinged feet moved back and forth over the worn wooden pedalboard. Her face glowed in the soft light from the music stand high above the three manuals of ivory keys. She nodded to her little visitor as she did each week, without missing a note.

It was very warm in the loft. The organ was a powerful but underserviced machine that bellowed slow beautiful tones, out of tune, but still causing a mighty stirring in the chest. The complex higher notes stormed out of the pipes. The floor of the loft vibrated from the sound. Some keys no longer sent atmosphere through its arteries to the corresponding pipes, but Betty knew which they were and skillfully avoided them. When she finished, the silence pushed on their ears. After a few minutes of whispered conversation, Amy said goodbye and scampered down the worn, unlit stairs.

She came out into the sunlight and pulled off her hat. The heat pushed down on the top of her head.

Outside of the church, a small group of parishioners remained, standing in somewhat of a line, chatting as they waited to each get a drink of ice-cold well water. Men laid their suit coats over their arms and loosened their ties. Ladies stood a few yards away in the shade of tall pine trees. Her father was waiting for her.

"Can we get a drink, Dad?"

He nodded yes, took her hand, and they joined the line.

When it was their turn, she took the little tin cup that dangled on a chain attached to the old hand pump.

"Now, I'll pump, and you scrub the cup real good," he said. "Keep your feet out of the water."

Amy leaned forward and held the metal cup under the pumping stream of water; it gushed and stopped, gushed and stopped as her father pumped. She rubbed the rim because everyone today had drunk from the same cup; in fact, anyone who had gotten a drink at church for a hundred years had used this cup. The water was clear and cold, and the tin cup set her teeth on edge. It was dented, and the rim was worn thin and smooth.

She filled it twice for herself before she filled it for her dad. He bent down to drink because the chain was short. He stretched back up tall. "Let's go home and make lunch!" he said. He smiled and asked her all about old Betty and the organ as they walked to the car.

Christmas Eve at the Market, 1967

As Amy and her dad came out of the cold and into the stuffy warm store, Mrs. C. was behind the counter as always. On a normal day, she would be nervously scrutinizing any children who milled around the candy display, sure that they would shoplift a pack of gum or a Chunky bar if she allowed her vigilance to falter. Today, she was smiling and was wearing a ruffled white apron embroidered with green holly leaves and red berries. Her pocket was stuffed with candy canes, and she gave one to each child.

Each time the door opened, the bells on the door jingled as they always did, but today, it seemed as though they rang more merrily, more gustily, more earnestly. It was Christmas Eve, and business was brisk at Catanese market in Warrendale. It was an old-fashioned Italian grocery, and Cuzzi Catanese and his son Gary were real butchers, with a case full of fine meats and cheeses in the deep sanctuary of the store. They held court behind the meat counter.

Many customers came in, shopped, paid, and left hurriedly, calling "Merry Christmas" as they hugged their bundles and shoved the door open with their elbows, trailing children sticky from the candy canes. Other customers came in who were not in a hurry but rather had a relaxed sense of liberation. With their Christmas Eve chores and duties done, or nearly so, they had come in to enjoy the hospitality of the small town's grocer. This was a happy tradition that Cuzzi had instituted and now kept each year.

At noon on December 24, the back of the store was transformed from meat counter to Italian bistro and country town meeting. There were festoons of sausage and wieners overhead, swirling around aging provolones. Behind the deli cases was a sanctum, which on this special day was filled with tables full of cheeses, breads, cured meats and olives, and towers of homemade Italian cookies. The ancient wooden butcher block was carefully wiped and oiled so it could double as a simple but robust bar. Red wine, whisky, or ouzo. Ginger ale. The bottles looked tipsy arranged on the worn rounded block and staggered a little each time they were picked up and slammed back down.

Cuzzi was perched on his throne, a tall stool next to the telephone and order pad, not far from the butcher block bar just in front of the big meat locker. He wore a clean white apron over his huge perfectly round belly instead of the meat-infused one he usually had on. He alternately poured drinks and popped slices of spicy capicola ham into his mouth.

The firemen from the volunteer fire department were there, housewives and children, farmers in checked wool shirts and overalls, which smelled like gasoline. Weaving in and out with trays of food were Gary's sisters and grandma; Art King, the assistant butcher; store hands sweeping up and carrying out larger orders. Harry Warren stood quietly near the door and nodded and smiled if anyone looked at him or said, "Hey, Harry, how ya doin?"

In the midst of the furor and festivity, customers would approach and yell, "Hey, Cuzzi, I need a pound of prosciutto," and he would descend from his stool astonishingly lightly, and in one motion deftly whipped open the glass case and heaved a ham onto the slicer with one hand. For every pound of meat, at least one slice made its way to his lips. His eyes twinkled, and he said, "Oh, you're going to like this."

So swiftly that you could almost not see his hands, he wrapped the meat in white paper, wrote the price, and laid it within the customer's reach between the rows of fresh turkeys atop the case. Each bird was lying on an open bed of white paper in a cardboard tray, a large fistful of parsley poking out, and a tag tied to a drumstick bearing the last name of one neighbor or another. While coaxing them to stay for a drink, he cleaned the slicer meticulously and replaced the ham in the case. His merry dance between the meat counter, the bar, and the tall stool went on as one by one, the turkeys disappeared; then the dusk would fall, and the store would close, and the last of the hangers-on would jingle out the front door.

The old-world smells and cries dovetailed naturally with the old building and its creaking wooden floors. This had been the first general store in Warrendale, next to the Fowlers Lumber on one side and the Brush Creek Inn on the other, the center of enterprise on Northgate Drive (Old Perry Highway) for 150 years. Families had owned it, grown old there, and moved on, followed by another family. There had been Warrens, and Fowlers, and Violas, and now Catanese.

Cuzzi scanned the mob and bellowed. "Bernie! Go back to the kitchen while Amy gets her cookies. We got something for you."

Bernie pushed aside the fabric curtain door and ducked through to the family quarters. Amy was happily grazing through meat and cheese and giggling with kids from school, still working her way up to anise cookies, biscotti, and cannoli. Later at home, they would all hear from Bernie about the Italian Christmas Eve fare that was in the kitchen. The Seven Hills of Rome, a table laden with seven kinds of fish, prepared in the old world style, for just the family and closest friends. He sampled clam chowder, squid and shrimp, swordfish, tuna, and anchovies.

After a while he reappeared and said, "Let's go, Ame. Mum's waiting for us." His cheeks were red and his eyes were merry. She hugged Cuzzi, and they made their way up to the front of the store. They paid for their groceries, and Mrs. C. gave her a candy cane to take home. She reached across the counter, smiled, and pinched Amy's arm.

"Have a nicey!" she said.

The Week That Was, 1965

Brownie camp sounded like it was going to be fun. Amy knew that Boy Scouts camped out, and although she knew little about what actually happened at a camp, she was sure it had to do with outdoors, tents, fires, hot dogs, swimming in lakes, singing; she liked all those things.

What she did not know was that little girls (Brownies) don't generally like the outdoors, tents, fires, lakes, and that Brownie leaders (grown-ups who used to be girls) planned things for the week of camping that involved those as little as possible.

Generally undaunted by difficulties, she was a child accustomed to taking things in stride. It was a time and culture that taught that hardship and setbacks were a part of life and that character was built by persevering. Brownie camp was one experience in which the disappointments ultimately outweighed the benefits; but sometimes, this too is a part of growing up.

The first day, much time was spent in a wooden building with a concrete floor, drawing pictures of flowers, tents, campfires, and lakes. The food was a lot like school food but not as good. The Brownies did go outside to collect flowers, which turned out to be disastrous for Amy. She found all the same wild flowers as the other little girls—chicory, Queen Anne's lace, and Jack-in-the-pulpit—but her bouquet was special because it had wonderful dark red, shiny ivy woven all through it. The Brownie leader gasped when she saw it, then scrubbed Amy's face with green soap and cheap paper towels in the hope of eviting the inevitable, but she still ended up in the hospital that night with eyes swollen shut. Accustomed to identifying poison ivy in full, lush, dark green leaf, she had been deceived by the young vines.

Lumpy, red, and itchy, she returned to camp the second day undaunted. She found that a little brook wound its way through the camp. It gurgled its way past the main meeting area and along a lonely path. She followed it into the woods. This harmless little stream playfully ducked under a small wooden foot bridge, and crouching low, so did she. Emerging on the other side, she stood up and connected soundly with a dangling board with a rusty nail adorning it. The laceration on her itchy left eye was expertly repaired at the hospital.

The third day was promising; the girls were going to build a fire and cook lunch on it. However, just as the smoke started to really smell like a camp fire, Ruth pulled up to the cabin in the old Dodge station wagon. Amy's grandfather had had a heart attack, and the whole family waited at the hospital together for the outcome. As it turned out, he recovered, and the biggest impression the visit made upon Amy was that the lady at the information desk knew them all by name; it was the third day in a row that they had been there.

One day, there was a swimming class. Not in the murky green lake but in a murky green swimming pool. Amy followed instructions and paddled furiously but could not bring herself to open her crusty poison ivy eyes. She was too worried about her stitches getting wet; she heard lots of yelling and finally opened her eyes. She had made her way all the way into the deep end of the pool. Little girls noticed this long before the instructor. Of course, she did not drown but rather choked, sputtered, and cried until rescued. Nothing would entice her back into the pool that day. To this day, she is a poor and nervous swimmer, given to squinting and hyperventilation as she stiffly doggy-paddles along. However, none of these departures from the intended joy of camping was as bad as the last.

It was the last day. Mrs. Taylor, a neighbor, had volunteered to drive to camp. Amy stood at the end of the driveway very early in the misty morning, waiting. She was gazing down Harmony Road and watching for the big blue Chevy. Out of the corner of her eye, she saw a tan object lying on the other side of the highway. Terrified of the cars whizzing past in whirlwinds of gravel and breaking every prohibition against it, she tiptoed across the highway. There was their beloved dog Buffer, his tan and white collie coat fluffy and still. His car death had been sudden and clean, a broken neck.

Mrs. Taylor was calling out to her from the shoulder of the road. Amy dashed and tottered back to Harmony Road. The frightened woman scooped her into her arms and into the safety of the big car. "My doggie, my doggie," Amy sobbed.

The poor woman wanted more than anything to stop the child's crying and distress. She did what so many grown-ups do when at a loss. She lied. "Oh honey, that's not your doggie. It's just a doggie that *looks* like your doggie!"

Time halted and so did the crying. Amy contemplated this for a moment as Mrs. Taylor put the car in gear and pulled out. Stunned into silence, scrutinizing the back of the woman's head, she watched her out of the corner of her good eye. Was she kidding? Blind? Was she right? It never entered her mind that Mrs. Taylor would be untruthful. Minutes passed. She could not argue with her; she is a grown-up and must know these things. By the time they got to the campground, Amy was sure that Mrs. Taylor must be right. That could not have been Buffer.

It was the last day of camp; she tried to have fun, and before she knew it, she saw her mother coming toward her at the end of the evening. Ruth's eyes were sad. At home, on the very top of the hill under the old pear tree, Amy found a mound of fresh earth adorned with a crude, boyish wooden cross that Bob had placed there. For the rest of the summer, she watched for her dog to come home. It was a long time before she stopped believing that Mrs. Taylor was right. Probably, some other similar dog was buried there, and her doggie would soon come home.

Oliver the Postmaster, 1969

Living on a hill, anywhere you go is "down." You go down to the store, down to the school, down to the post office.

Halfway through dinner, the phone rang. When Bernie hung up, he said, "That was Oliver. The berry plants are here. I told him I'd be right down."

He finished his last few bites quickly; he knew that the postmaster was waiting for him and would not lock up the post office and walk home until Bernie came for his strawberry plants. Oliver didn't heat the place at night; it was the first week of March, and the little plants would freeze—all ten thousand of them. And the crates would be in the way in the morning anyhow.

"Come on, Ame. Dress warm," he said.

The post office looked weird at night, with just the back lights on. Amy had never been there at night, never come in the back door, had never been on the other side of the wall of mail boxes.

In the daytime, when they came for their mail, they entered the little front door, stamped their feet on the wooden plank floor, and went up to the wall of post office boxes like everyone else. The doors on the numbered mailboxes looked strong and secure, heavy glass and detailed brass, all scrolled and worn shiny. Each post office box lock had two perfect little knobs, which turned smoothly and silently as you worked your secret combination that enabled only you to open the box. "207," the heavy brass plate said in elegant Gothic letters. The door opened on sturdy hinges and revealed a sleek compartment holding daily surprises. There would be magazines, and letters, envelopes of all different sizes and colors, sometimes with money or a stick of gum from Aunt Orie.

To Amy's amazement, the wall of boxes was very different from Oliver's side. The mailboxes were just open in the back, unguarded receptacles, with a plain number stamped on the wood above each one. The floor was wooden and worn slick into a trough behind the wall of boxes. The tiny back room was crowded, holding only a small table with a cash register and black telephone that worked, an old telegraph that didn't, two canvas bins labeled "IN" and "OUT." A heavy black safe decorated with gold scrolled lines that said, "Stamps," was under the postal window. There was a solitary coat hook for the postmaster next to the door (the door that could barely be gotten through because every inch of space in the post office was filled with wooden crates of strawberry plants).

Mr. Oliver looked different too. Amy was accustomed to seeing his gleaming bald head, adorned by his shiny visor, but there he stood, visorless, and wearing a furry black hat.

"Have fun, Bern," chuckled Mr. Oliver. "I'll take twenty quarts of berries next year."

He held the door as Bernie carried crate after crate out and loaded them into the station wagon. Snowflakes swirled around the little building's back door in the car headlights. After locking up carefully, Oliver trudged the few hundred feet to the hedges that separated the postal lot from his yard and disappeared.

At home, the crates were unloaded and lined up against the foundation of the house near the water spigot. Bernie pried them open with a crowbar. "Can I go inside now, Dad? It's freezing out here."

He laughed. "We're not done yet, Ame. Start pulling the bundles off the top layer, and I'll water the ones underneath. Loosen the little ties around each bundle a little."

She wished Bob was not in the Army, not in Vietnam, and was here to do the berries.

There were twenty-five plants to a bundle, five hundred plants in a crate, twenty crates in all. To little cold red fingers, the task seemed endless. She loosened the ties. Each bundle had a head full of tiny green leaves and long gray roots she could barely get her hands around. She held them as her father lovingly gave each bundle a drink. The water from the well was icy cold, and after the first crate, their hands were numb.

Amy was delighted when they were all watered, and the wet straw was packed back around them. Then her dad said, "We have to cover them up now so they don't freeze." Together they went and got stacks of newspapers and horse blankets from the garage. They were heavy, itchy, and smelled faintly like horses which had been gone for a few years.

As they layered them over the berry crates in the dark, Amy tried to remember if she really liked strawberries that much. She began to reflect on how much work there soon would be, putting ten thousand plants in the ground, and all without Bob.

A few days later, she was in the bright post office, spinning the dials to unlock number 207. Oliver peeked out at her from behind the bars of his official postal window. He smiled and asked her, "How's berry farming?"

"Cold," she said and felt very grown up making conversation with the postmaster.

Mrs. Wick, 1963

Mrs. Wick was born early in the twentieth century and was teaching in a one room school by the time she was twenty. In her fourth decade of teaching, she stood in front of her Marshall Elementary third grade class as motivated and dedicated as any teacher and far better educated and experienced than most.

Her blouse was white with ruffles at the neck and bust, a pencil-straight navy blue skirt fell below her knees. Although her ankles were thick, they were not swollen or painful looking. She wore sensible low navy shoes.

Her hair was striped black and silver, twisted femininely into a chignon. Gold-rimmed glasses on a neck swag of cut glass beads drifted around in the billowy white ruffles, now and then catching a sparkle of light. She was beautiful and serious in a way that said, "I expect the best of myself and therefore everyone else, including you," to her students.

In those days, a third grade teacher had her flock of twenty-five nine-year-olds in her room all day and taught them all subjects, except for art, music, and physical education. For those subjects, as well as assemblies, the whole class marched down the basement steps to the gymatorium. It was really just a large room with a polished tile floor. Chairs and large folding tables were brought from their resting places against the walls on art days. Mats hung on the walls at the ready for gymnastics and tumbling.

In the boiler room were a screen and movie projector for filmstrips, a pommel horse for gymnastics, and two eight-foot wooden risers the sixth grade chorus stood on for Christmas and spring concerts. These items were brought out of the boiler room when needed to enrich the children's education or when the room was needed so the children could practice being bombed by communists. It had the feel of a bomb shelter, even when the projector was clicking out a National Geographic filmstrip.

It was comforting to go back upstairs to "homeroom." Homeroom was aptly named, for it was where friends were met, boots and coats were kept, lunch was eaten. It was the anchor for a young child setting sail each day on the stormy sea of social and academic life. The teacher's desk was a bench of justice and an oasis of reassurance, the seat of authority, access to the one in charge. The large desk had a permanent feeling. It was adorned with texts and supplies, a cup of tall, clean yellow pencils with perky pink erasers, which called to mind cut flowers. A bronze paper-weight and the teacher's drinking cup were two personal items that never varied. Her gloves (sometimes white, sometimes taupe), a lace handkerchief (she didn't say "hanky"), and a black umbrella were the only other things that ever resided there not having to do with school work.

Enormous windows that stretched from the radiator shelf to the twelve-foot ceiling provided light, air, and a view of the Pennsylvania turnpike just beyond the play yard. Two streams of cars and trucks flowed past in opposite directions. There were long pauses between vehicles, during which the sighing white pines and tall oaks on the other side of the pike soothed a child whose attention had wandered outside.

Mrs. Wick believed that education should prepare one for life outside the classroom. Actions, words, and ideas all had consequences. A day in her class provided dozens of opportunities to practice the skills and use the knowledge she doled out. She created a post office and postal system. Each child brought a shoebox and was given a post office box number. Each week, one student was appointed as postmaster, and he or she placed mail in the boxes. This mail was comprised of graded homework, notes from the teacher with advice or encouragement, and letters between students (which had to be written longhand), and even report cards. The postmaster kept the post office tidy and dispensed postage stamps, which the students earned by cleaning the erasers and chalkboard, sweeping the floor, extracredit assignments, and exemplary behavior. The post office was situated in one corner of the room. It was open during lunch, recess, and before school in the morning during homeroom. Students had a duty to check their mail every day.

A librarian was selected each week to manage the class library, which was in another corner of the room and circulated classics suitable for all levels of readers age nine or ten, a Bible, a dictionary, periodicals and novels, and sheet music for those who played an instrument. Mrs. Wick had assembled this collection herself through the years and populated it with books she loved. The little librarian checked books and materials and organized the shelves.

Another coveted job was milkman, who distributed cartons of milk and collected the nickels. The trash collector went ceremoniously to each desk at the end of lunch period and collected the refuse in a bag.

These positions each paid two postage stamps per week, and every student had the chance to work them an equal number of days per school year. The library and post office created an orderly and fun economy in which students took pride. Valentines choked the little boxes in February. Birthday greetings were sent, party invitations and other important missives, without ever disturbing the academic environment. Boys and girls rarely misbehaved; they were occupied, engaged, and in pursuit of postage!

Mrs. Wick read aloud to the class every day at lunch. Meals were brought from home as there was no cafeteria. As brown bags and a few metal lunch boxes were brought out of the desks and opened, milk was distributed by that day's appointed milk-man. After all trading of apples, pickles, and candy was settled, children chewed quietly so as not to miss a word of her eloquent readings. After twenty minutes, she would close the book, saying, "What do you think is going to happen next?" and they all tried to guess.

Recess followed. Fair weather meant twenty minutes to run, swing on the swing set, and play kickball. Girls would congregate in front of the wings of the War Memorial and talk; boys would pick holly berries and pitch them over the memorial onto the girls. By fifth grade, girls would celebrate recess by walking arm in arm in a loop around the building. Fifth- and sixth-grade boys would stand in groups at the corners talking, playing with pocket knives, or throwing a ball against the brick wall. They pretended to ignore the girls as they made their circuit.

Recess indoors meant post office, library, checkers, or jacks; boys who had milked or done other farm work before school dozed at their desks while others simply talked and gazed out at gray rain or blue snow punctuated by headlights sliding by in yellow-white pairs. Then, when the bell rang, quiet resumed as Mrs. Wick brought each school subject to life.

She was especially capable of animating history for them. Amy thought that this was probably because Mrs. Wick had lived through so much of it.

One day, she was talking about pioneer days. The teacher strived to impress upon the children what hardships the pioneers had endured. She explained that even at the time she was born, many people still lived without the modern comforts that the students enjoyed.

"In the past, there were many homes that did not have running water or indoor plumbing. Rain water was collected in rain barrels or carried from a spring. People in the past heated their homes with wood-burning stoves or fireplaces. Before homes had electricity, candles or lamps provided light."

Amy raised her hand. Mrs. Wick paused. "Yes, Amy, do you have a question?"

"I just wanted to tell you that the past is still happening," she said.

"Why, what do you mean, dear?" Her eyes twinkled; she was intrigued.

"I go to a place where the past is still happening all the time! It's called Guffy. Aunt Orie lives there, and it used to be my great-grandmother's house," she explained. "We cook on a coal stove, and there isn't a bathroom, and they don't have a car!"

Mrs. Wick let Amy tell the class about Guffy. She asked questions about the family life there. She deftly wove the contribution into her lesson. Any time a child was able to participate, she made them feel important, a partner in education.

Then, others spoke up, telling of similar experiences right in their own homes, revealing that some of them lived where the past was still happening.

July Fourth Parade, 1969

Being Bonnie Fowler's friend had perks. First of all, you had many opportunities to play with fire. Since the Fowler Homestead had no central heat, the kitchen was heated by the four gas burner rings on the stove, which burned at full jet all winter. In most rooms, there were fireplaces to burn wood, paper, garbage, notes from the teacher, report cards, and anything else two child pyromaniacs could find. In the bathroom was a gas heater, which was great fun because it had to be lit with matches. There was also a large gas heater in the parlor with decorative grates that threw exotic shadows on the high ceiling and walls at night, when the two little girls slept in there on antique divans and chaises, especially fun when candles were also added to the mix.

Another benefit of being welcomed into the Fowler homestead house was that Bonnie's mother was detached, and her father was rarely home because he worked and was chief of the fire department. This meant lots of freedom—no interference from parents, no bedtimes, no food rules (in fact, very little food), and above all, no accountability for whereabouts or activities.

They could spend hours in the abandoned barn, in the woods, at the creek, in the summer kitchen (more fire making opportunities), or even walk to town, and no one ever questioned them or even noticed if they came or went.

Bonnie had a citizens band radio. She and Amy could stay up all night talking to truck drivers and other *CB*ers. Wrapped in old blankets, they cooked anything they had on the fireplace, learning about everything from what the truckers may be hauling to how tough and lonely it was for a fellow to be on eighteen wheels.

Grandpa Fowler was also a plus. At 102, he was blind, totally deaf, toothless, incontinent, ambulatory, and very opinionated. His name was William, and his great nephew Ken, who was Bonnie's father, was his caregiver.

William had been a pillar of the community and well into the twentieth century, ran the general store and the lumber businesses his father had established during the 1800s.

Bonnie also cared for him, and when she was there, Amy helped. The two little girls would help him to cook and eat, but he did almost everything else himself. Ken had rigged most of the house with chain handrails screwed to the old oak wainscot, and William followed the chains safely to the bathroom or the porch or his bed. He talked to himself, quiet loudly, which lent an eerie quality to the rattling sound of his chain-supported travels through the old house at night.

In the mornings, Bonnie and Amy would go to the orchard or the old barn. The barn was a museum, frozen in the moment it had become unused. At some time in the 1940s, the horses and cattle were sold and an automobile came to the farmstead. No one had bothered to take away the lanterns, pitchforks, leather tack, sleigh fixtures, buckets, and barrels. The long-abandoned artifacts stood like stage properties in the still morning light, and the only thing that moved were motes of dust in the air.

The sun warmed a large bright square on the board floor, and the two little brown haired girls sat there. They had a breakfast of elderberries picked in the early dew. When they were not talking or giggling, the only sound was the occasional creaking or sighing of old beams.

The girls were trying to figure out why "blondes have more fun." The television commercials which stated this seemed very author-itative to them. They had presented this concern to their mothers, convinced that the purveyors of hair bleach had their best interest in mind. Neither mother was convinced that the little girls needed to have more fun, and even if they did, peroxide surely would not provide it.

They had petitioned Mrs. Barren, who owned the drugstore, but she was adamant in her refusal to conspire against their parents. So on this sunny day, they had walked to the market, and instead of buying their usual ration of penny candy, had obtained two lem-ons. It was believed that lemon juice and sunshine could produce a remarkable lightening of dull, un-fun brunette hair. After a few hours of rubbing and combing lemon juice into rather stiff hairdos, the only effect was a very red and freckled sunburn on each little face.

It seemed as though lying in the stream at the bottom of the backfield would cheer them up, and so it did. Minnows were caught and released. Hunger drove them into the orchard for some apples, which were just ripening. Eventually, the last hour of the afternoon was filled with playing with matches, cuddling the new kittens in the summer kitchen, and talking about things they loved.

It had been a great summer. The Fourth of July parade had been a red letter day for them and served for good conversational material. Because Bonnie's father was fire chief, he planned and led the Independence Day parade. He drove the big fire engine, which was a vintage pumper, with ladders and hoses coiled and stacked on the roof.

Ken had the wonderful idea of dressing Bonnie and Amy up as clowns and perching them atop the fire truck, with huge bags of candy to fling out to the bystanders as the parade moved past. Ever safety conscious, Ken had tied them to the top of the truck, just behind the siren, with clothesline.

Wearing hot, curly, neon-colored wigs and polka dotted costumes, they sat to have their makeup applied. Faces painted white, Bonnie with a hideous red frown and Amy with an equally hideous grin, they waved their arms and threw candy the length of the parade route. The starting point was easy to spot; there was a colorful knot of wooden sawhorses wrapped with crepe paper and a few riders perched on nervous horses glancing white-eyed at the fire trucks.

The route was from the fire hall to the end of Northgate drive (half a mile in length) and back. The truck was followed by the drum and bugle corps, called the Boots and Saddles, which was a small herd of teenagers wearing cowboy hats and befringed and booted in black and gold; the Boy and Girl Scouts of America; then the tractors, red and green like Christmas; followed by the Veterans of Foreign War; and brought up at the rear by Doctor Etter on horseback. The parade made strategic stops in front of the post office and Brush Creek Inn and Marshall Elementary School. The crowd sang the national anthem in front of the school while facing the veterans monument.

When the parade was over, the two clowns were stripped of their rented glory and became little girls again. They crawled around on the floor of the fire hall and lay under the fire trucks on the cool cement. The firemen and their families sat in the call room and drank beer and laughed. After a while, the band for the square dance arrived and began to set up. The square dance callers brought a microphone and amplifier.

Soon, all of the fire trucks were pulled out and parked on the street to make room for the square dance. The third graders were excited. Square dancing was taught in gym class starting in third grade, so this would be the first time to actually participate in a real dance.

When the music started, many couples immediately took their places. Among the younger set, girls waited expectantly for someone to bow and put out his hand in invitation. Age was not an issue; many grandpas and firemen as well as school boys partnered girls who seemed willing to dance. It was a polite and fun time.

How fast it went! The experienced dancers helped and coached the newest, and everyone flowed together smoothly. Hand met hand; smile met smile. The callers were clear and lively and skillfully wove in the first names of many of the old timers.

Before Amy knew it, the dance was over. Her feet were sore and blistered from dancing on the concrete fire hall floor, but she didn't mind. She ran out into the dark parking lot to cool off and found a large bunch of kids from school. They decided to walk to the school and back.

She found herself walking next to Eddie, a sixth grade boy who was tall and quiet and very funny. He asked her for a kiss.

"If you climb the flag pole at the school, I will," she said.

"Why, I will. Just you watch!"

Off he ran.

The whole group arrived at the front of the school. It was totally dark, except for the moon. They stood around the pole and looked up, watching Eddie shimmy up the pole.

"I did it!" he yelled and slid all the way down. "I'll collect that kiss now."

Amy closed her eyes, and he kissed her very respectfully. The others cheered and laughed. It was an innocent and happy Fourth of July first kiss.

CHAPTER 4

Guffy Hollow

Not only am I the youngest to remember our family living there, but I am also surely the youngest and last to have loved Guffey Hollow. The house and those who lived there were wild, mysterious, and primitive. Their grandparents were Scots, Indians, and French.

The old people who were my history told us stories of hardship, laughter, wars, coal miners, gambling, and even anarchists who lived a little way back in the hollow and who plotted to murder President McKinley. I did not know until 1990 that the anarchists were real; I found the newspaper account online. I have no reason not to believe all the other stories as well.

My parents took my brother and me and carloads of provisions up into the hollow for long weekends, summer, and winter. We took tools, paint buckets, and brushes and loved the house. We took fresh strawberries. We took delight in the silent loneliness. I loved Guffy. It surely should have been mine.

The Coal Stove, 1961

The coal bucket was full and very heavy. The metal pail handle cut grooves into her fingers and made the tips numb. The bucket bumped against each of the narrow wooden cellar steps. Amy tried to lift it high enough to clear each riser. She knew she was making too much noise so early in the morning. She was determined to do a good job.

Aunt Orie had wakened her up while everyone else was still asleep. "Do you want to make breakfast with me on the coal stove, girl?"

Her creased face looked just as severe as usual, but Amy could see that Aunt Orie thought this would be fun. It was a special invitation. So the five-year-old jumped out of her warm nest of covers, and in the half-light, she could see the sparkling frost on the floor. Aunt Orie was wearing a black sweater over her dress, clasped in the front with a silver chain. Amy hurried into clothing that was stiff with cold.

Cooking was interesting to Amy. Food was important and festive and a big part of any family that grew food. This was even more interesting. How do you cook on a coal stove? There are no control knobs to turn the heat up and down. And there is so much more to do before you can even start the food. But fire was fascinating and… warm!

So they opened the door to where the coal went and stirred the last glowing embers from last night. They had to slowly add coal at the beginning. After the flu was adjusted and as things started to heat up, they could drop more coal in.

You had to be careful not to lean against the hottest parts of the stove. You had to fill the water bottle on the side. You had to adjust the draft. You had to carry more water. It was getting nice and warm in the kitchen. Aunt Orie dipped her rag into icy water from the rain barrel and scrubbed Amy's face till it was red and the coal smudges were gone.

Soon, a huge black iron fry pan, filled with thick bacon, began to sizzle. When the bacon was done, Orie dumped big white kernels of hominy into the grease and fried them till they were golden. And last of all, a dozen eggs were slid into the smooth black skillet, and while they cooked, bread was toasted right on the top of the stove. Amy was sent to the pantry for jam and chili sauce.

Coffee boiled in a speckled enamel percolator. All of the smells combined and crept up the back stairs to gently awaken everyone. In pajamas and bathrobes or in full dress, they ambled one by one through the kitchen. Some went outside to the little necessary house perched in the snow. Uncle Tom went downstairs to stoke the coal furnace. Everyone came back into the warm kitchen, pulled coffee mugs from their hooks, and huddled around the stove and its crown jewel, the speckled enamel coffee pot.

Amy was proud to be in the kitchen, stirring things and helping when they all came down. It felt like a rite of passage as a young lady, even though she didn't name the feeling. Her mother noticed and silently smiled approval.

Aunt Orie chased everyone away from the stove.

"How the hell am I supposed to serve breakfast. Get to the table."

They all laughed at her gruffness and settled in at the ancient claw-foot table. There was a lot of chatter and a lot of food. It was the most delicious breakfast Amy would ever taste.

The Rain Barrel, 1963

Outside Amy's car window, the world was a black-and-white movie. Pale snowflakes fell from a pewter sky and outlined the black tree trunks. Forty feet below the tiny winding track, a gray stream choked with enormous black rocks rushed deeply between white banks. She had to strain her neck to see down into the gorge.

The soundtrack of this movie was not music; it was the sound of chains. Her father had turned the radio off when he steered their 1957 Chevy off the main road onto the Guffy Hollow road. He had pulled over, gotten out, and in the Friday evening gloom put the tire chains on. "Chuffle, chuffle, chuffle," said the tires. No one spoke.

There was steam on the windows. Bernie drove slowly, wiping the inside of the windshield now and then with his hanky.

They did not see another car; in fact, their tires were the first to mar the deep wet snow, silvery in their headlights. This was the only road into the hollow. They would pass only one house. In a few miles, the Tuglavini's house appeared on the right, on the far side of the creek. They crept by it slowly. A half mile further in, a tall frame house stood alone. It stood stark against the steep mountainside, against which it nestled. Smoke billowed out of the two chimneys from the kitchen coal stove and from the coal furnace.

Bernie picked up a little speed, ramped up into the front yard, and stopped. There was snow piled up in front of the radiator. After the long drive, it seemed very quiet in the car. Amy knew she would not hear the sound of another machine until they left on Sunday evening.

She opened her door and got out into snow above her knees. She waited as the rest of the family began wading toward the house about fifty yards away. When the front door banged shut, she looked at the house and saw her father coming back for her.

They stood there together in the silent blue-gray light for a few minutes just listening. Something stirred in her chest. There was a deep, mighty quiet, filled with the sound of thousands of naked trees sighing in unison. Her father gazed at her, and she realized that he was deeply satisfied that they shared this moment. She took his hand, and they struggled to the house together.

It was hot in the kitchen, and Aunt Orie was standing by the coal stove stirring boiling potatoes. She gave one the feeling that she had been standing right there cooking for a hundred years. She cooked on this stove winter and summer. As Amy took off her coat and put her boots by the big black stove, she thought about the way Orie did things. This winter night, the heat was welcome. But even in August, she would make Sunday dinner—roast beef, potatoes, beans, hominy grits—and it would be nearly one hundred degrees in there by the time they sat down to eat on a summer day.

On days like that, after dinner, there would be the pleasure of seeking relief from the heat to fill a long afternoon. In the immediate-past-summer, Amy had stood around on the once-proud-but-now-sagging wooden porch until she was sure that none of the grownups were coming out. She leaned against the cool rough side of the rain barrel. It came up just to her armpits. Her fingertips dipped into the water, which she was forbidden to touch. It was intended for bathing and washing. *Just up to my elbows*, she thought.

Her arms found their way into the barrel. The rim burnt her underarms. She pushed up and balanced on the metal edge, which was very uncomfortable. She felt better with her legs in the water.

It was only a moment until she was in the barrel. It was cool and still. Amy inched down in up to her nostrils. There was a green lakey smell to the soft still water. While she was thinking about hippos and alligators, her bare feet encountered the slime on the bottom of the barrel. She pressed against the warm sides with her hands and feet and felt her dress flutter around her.

Her brother's voice next to her ear startled her. "Ame! What are you doin' in there?" he whispered. "You're gonna get spanked!"

She couldn't move. Had he not discovered her, she wondered, how would I have gotten out?

Bob hauled her out of the rain barrel, scraping the edge a little, and set her down gently. "You better go play somewhere till you're dry," he said.

Off and on for the rest of the day, he would occasionally look at her and mouth the words, "I'm telling," but she knew he was teasing.

The water from the rain barrel had to be carried in buckets to the kitchen and poured into a round metal tub when it was time to take a bath. This particular winter evening, there had been ice on the barrel an inch thick to break through. It took a long time to heat the water, and Aunt Orie had Bob shovel more coal into the stove, and it was roaring. A small flannel nightgown was spread on a chair pulled close, as well as a clean rough towel that smelled like bleach.

Amy's mother, Ruth, was sitting with her feet up on the shelf on the side of the coal stove, and her aunt sat in the high-backed kitchen chair, and as they smoked, Amy was sitting in the tub, wishing the water was warmer. She knew that it was going to be very cold upstairs, and the hundred-year-old linen sheets would be cold too. However, she loved the sheets, which were crisp, dense, rough, and wonderful. There were feather pillows, and the pillowcases were also pure heavy linen, embroidered with flowers by hands of relatives long dead.

For the second time that day, the little girl met the eyes of a grown-up gazing at her. Aunt Orie usually spoke to children only when they needed instruction or to be scolded. Tonight, she said, "I have something for you." Her big brown eyes were soft and nostalgic.

She left for a moment, and when she returned, she had a square, silk-covered box in her hands. It was ancient looking but in perfect condition. It was figured with tiny blossoms that gleamed in the lamplight. Orie pulled her chair closer to Amy and sat with the box in her lap. Her white hair was up in a bun as always. Deep creases ran from the corners of her mouth, which held only a few teeth. Ruth poured some more hot water into the tub as Orie opened the box and began to tell a story. It was a story she had chosen to tell only once or twice in her whole life.

"When I was girl, we lived in the city of Allegheny. My parents took us out of the hollow so we could go to school. But I was only a little older than you when I went to work at a box factory. Not cardboard boxes, mind you. Back then, they were made of wood.

"I was proud to make a little money, and I gave it all to my mother. But sewing was what I loved, and I dreamed of being a dressmaker. The finest ladies had their dresses made for them in those days. But it was only a dream. Making boxes not only ruined my hands but my education as well. The summer after I finished third grade, I went to work. I was angry and bitter.

"I started to smoke cigarettes. It was the only pleasure in my life. After work, as we all waited for the train, we would talk and smoke."

Amy was shivering in the metal tub full of lukewarm water. Her Aunt had never talked to her this much before, and Amy was wondering what any of this had to do with the little silk box.

"Oh, for God's sake," Orie muttered, "the kid is freezing." She got up, went to the coal stove, and found more water, almost boiling. Carrying it to the tub, she held her cigarette in her mouth and squinted her eyes against the smoke as she poured it in near Amy's feet.

"Swirl it, girl."

After she sat down, Orie resumed the story.

"Time goes by," she said and glanced at Ruth.

"Don't it!" she laughed.

"Well, when I was seventeen, I met a young man. He was goin' a soldier in the Big War. It was 1916, and I got pregnant. When I told the folks, my pop threw me outside the door. My mother opened it again and threw out my hat and coat. In the pocket was fifty cents, enough for the train. I only had one place to go—Guffy Hollow.

"When I got here, Aunt Jane dried my nose and put me to bed. She found my young man and made him marry me right out by the roses. This box of soap is what he gave me for a wedding present. He was gone in a few weeks. He sent me his paychecks. He was killed in Europe before my baby came. Then whooping cough came to the hollow, I don't know how. My little girl was not quite two when she died.

"Aunt Jane saved my life. She delivered my baby. Then she taught me how to sew. Eventually, she found me a job in McKeesport as a seamstress. She walked me down the hollow to the train tracks and flagged down the train. We called it The Bummer because the conductor never made me pay to ride.

"I swore to her that I would always take care of her and of Guffy Hollow. This is the house that my grandfather built. He left it to her as a reward for her years as an indentured servant in Scotland. Her servitude had paid for the whole family's crossing to America. When she died, this place became mine."

More hot water was poured into the tub, and finally, the box was opened. The fragrance of apple blossoms wafted up from two little rows of the most delicate pink bars of soap. One of the tiny bars was placed into Amy's wrinkled fingers. As she began to wash with this fifty-year-old treasure, Orie spoke again.

"I never left the hollow again."

The details of that story, which was so rarely told, did not interest the little bather as much as the scent of the delicious soap. But a day would come when she would regret not paying more attention to the teller and the telling, regret not asking more about the war, the baby, the train. By the time Amy was old enough to realize what a gift the telling was, it was too late. Orie was gone. The box remains, and now and then, Amy still opens the little silk lid and breathes in the appleblossom breaths from the very last century-old bar of soap, and that long-ago winter evening flickers for a second into reality again.

Aunt Orie

The Green Rolling Pin, 1975

Aunt Orie's hands were transparent and wavered just a little as she presented the enormous old rolling pin to Amy. She tenderly touched the green handles before she let go. But giving it to Amy made her feel better. Leaving almost everything else in her home of seventy-six years felt like leaving her arms and legs behind. The tall curved breakfront china closet, the piano, the bed in which she was born and her only child had died in all had to be left. She had to say goodbye to the ancient coal stove that had been her friend and some-times master for much of her life. Too old to carry water and shovel coal, too poor to pay to have them delivered, too remote and stub-born to have modern improvements made, Orie was submitting to realities she had battled for decades. She was moving to Warrendale to live with her niece Ruth and her husband, Bernie.

They had a nice place with a few acres. It was one of the original Warrendale houses. Bernie was adding on to the old farmhouse for Orie and Bob, Ruth's father. She could take a few treasured things to the small apartment. Others she gave to Ruth's daughter Amy, the only one in that generation who seemed to care. Amy listened to the family stories.

"My mother, Anna Priscilla Watt, who was your great-grand-mother, had a sister Sarah Jane. Aunt Jane didn't sail with the family to America. She came eight years later. When she arrived at the house my grandfather built in Guffy Hollow, she was bitter and quiet and never told anyone what her life had been like as an indentured ser-vant. Her silence accused her parents and siblings.

"My mother married an American, who was Indian and French, named Covert, while Aunt Jane was still in Scotland. Grandpa had sold all their belongings and seven years of Sarah's life to pay passage for the whole family. He brought just a few things along. I'm giving your mother the round oak claw-foot table from my kitchen, and you get the brown ceramic door stop shaped like a dog. It was one hundred years old when he carried it here to Guffy in 1830.

"My mother had sixteen brothers and sisters. They were all raised here on this bend of the Youghiogheny River. When I was your age, people called us Scots, frogs, half-breeds, or Appalachians. Some of my uncles, the oldest boys, died in the Civil War. Some moved away. Some just died. A few were younger and worked in the coal mines. The girls grew food, mended, and scrubbed. Sarah Jane was an old maid by the time she was freed and came to America. Her life here must have seemed like a similar servitude to the one she left.

"Among those uncles who remained at home was Jim. Arrogant, lazy, and selfish, he spent his time playing poker up at the band hall near the big road, drinking and generally trying to terrorize his sisters and break Mommy's heart. My brother Tom is a lot like him.

"Aunt Jane managed the gardens and planted corn and made hominy. She grew, picked, and dried the corn. She soaked the kernels in lye till they swelled up, then tied them in sacks and laid them in the stream out back under the footbridge until the lye washed out. It would be dried then and ground into grits. When I came to the Hollow, that became my job. But now, we buy hominy in a can and grits in a box.

"This rolling pin with green handles belonged to my grandma; the color was a little bit of cheer in a plain home. Mommy and Aunt Jane took pride in their pies. Pastry made with lard, filled with meats or berries, squash, or grapes in season were pushed through the oven by the dozen. Early each morning, they were set out on a long board on the front porch to cool. I remember them bein' golden and full. They were a mainstay of the table, along with beans and potatoes."

Orie handed the green handled rolling pin to Amy. "Aunt Jane didn't get along with Uncle Jim. I'm going to tell you a story to remember once in a while when you are making pies!"

I See We Baked Pies Today, 1888

Jim swaggered into and through the kitchen one morning with hat and walking stick in hand. He eyed his sister Sarah Jane, tendrils of sweat-dampened hair around her narrow puckered face, flour on her apron, red rough hands carrying one of the day's pies. She quietly set the pie in the long row cooling on the porch shelf. He was seized with a malicious desire to punish her for being so good.

Whap, whap, whap, whap. His stick crashed down into each lovely pie; fruit and meat and steam poured out. "I…see…we… baked…pies…today," he said, emphasizing each word with a blow to another pie.

Sarah screamed and rushed at him with the rolling pin, but he was already out the door, laughing, and sprinting across the yard he escaped up the hollow. She stood for a moment, resigned and dumb, rolling pin dangling from one hand by her side. Her shoulders slumped a little lower. She sighed and walked back into the kitchen. There was work to do.

One night, not long after, Jim didn't come home. The next morning, some men knocked on the door and spoke in low tones to their father through the door. Grandpa took a wagon up to the band hall and returned with Jim's body in pieces. Jim was a gambler, and he cheated. He had been caught and tied to horses and drawn till quartered. He succeeded in breaking his mother's heart.

Eventually, Sarah Jane's parents died, and all the others were gone. When her sister married and moved to Allegheny City, Sarah was alone in the hollow. It was quiet and no one told her what to do.

Jip, 1909

"Tom, let him down! Please let him get down!" Orie pleaded with her brother. She could see him smiling and peeking at her out of the corner of his eye. Jip was panting, and his little black and white body weaved from side to side. It had been half an hour since Tom had commanded the dog to sit up and beg, and Jip dutifully held his pose, little paws in front. He quivered from fatigue and also fear. Jip knew that if he came down before Tom released him, he would get a terrible beating.

Orie thought about trying to kick Tom, but it would only give him a reason to run off down the hollow and leave the little dog. One time, Tom had left him like that, and they had all pleaded with Jip to lie down, but he would not. They tried to lure him with a morsel of meat. They tried to forcibly put him onto the ground, but he would scramble back up. He had finally tumbled over in the dark, and then hid in terror for a day or two till he was sure Tom had forgotten about him.

The Box Factory, 1910

Orie had been making wooden boxes since her tenth birthday, and now her little brother Bob wanted to work too. He had just finished the fifth grade. He had two more years of schooling than she, but she was older and smarter.

"Now don't say anything unless they ask you a question," she warned him. She had misgivings about taking him to work because he was stupid, and if he made a lot of mistakes, it wouldn't look good for her. But she also knew he would work hard, and Mommy needed the money. You didn't have to be very clever to make a box, just strong and careful. The sides came out of the punch room all cut. You had to knock them together with a mallet, sliding the bottom in as you pulled the sides all together. It was easier in winter when the wood was dry, but then you had splinters and cold hands.

It was 1910, and this year they would start to get a penny for every six boxes they assembled. That made it easier to bear; it made it possible to make sixteen cents a day, if you could make twelve an hour. Five minutes to get the wood, assemble it, soak it in the trough, and stack it. You could make ninety-six boxes in eight hours if you didn't have to go to the latrine. She was proud that the Heinz plant used their boxes. The boxes were sent to the strip district of Pittsburgh full of goods. After they went to the strip and were purchased by grocers and hotels, the sturdy boxes were useful in homes for a lot of things and eventually became kindling.

Bob got the job, and he was proud and happy. He had been stuck in school till the fifth grade, longer than any of the others, because he was the baby. He would show them how hard he could work; he was almost twelve, after all. And best of all, he would now make some money so he could buy his own tobacco to roll instead of stealing from Tom.

In the Coal Mine, 1957

Uncle Tom had yellow teeth, yellow-gray hair, and yellow tobacco-stained fingers. In the lamplight from his miner's cap the deep wrinkles which scored his ancient cheeks, and the bags under his eyes were black as coal. Tom was taking his great nephew into the mine for the first time. When he turned his back and walked away from Bobby, he was a black silhouette like the plywood cutouts people place in their yards at Halloween. The beam of his lamp sawed back and forth across dusty rock walls. They were dry and brown, with an occasional shiny black stripe.

To the boy, the walls of the mine shaft resembled marble cake. Tom was carrying a pick and shovel. "Push that car, boy! We gotta get coal," he snarled. It was a small wooden coal car guided by tiny rails. It had been there for seventy years and was rickety and reluctant. Smaller lumps leaked out of the corners. Bobby did not know how far in the tracks went or how far Tom would make him go. He was forbidden to be here at all. This heightened his terror of the man and the place.

Had Bernie and Ruth known that Bobby went in the mine, he thought that he would have been in big trouble. So he never told them; he made sure they didn't know. He was an adult before he realized that he had prevented his parents from protecting him from the mean old man and the danger of the mine.

The coal they brought out was not very good, but it filled the need in late March and early April when the good coal that had been delivered last fall ran out, and the Guffy hollow road was still impassable for a coal truck.

Bobby was tired and mentally exhausted by the time Tom released him. He played outside in the snow until you couldn't tell he had ever been dusty. He went inside, carrying a load of resentment that no one even knew he had gotten the coal. In a strange way, he also treasured the experience so fraught with fear and the feeling of having done something dangerous and secret.

The Guffy Piano, 1962

The parlor was the farthest room from the sanctuary of the warm kitchen. The heat of the coal stove, the sounds of grown-ups talking, the smell of smoke from their cigarettes were all distant and muted. The parlor was perfectly still and was a last resort for a child to stave off boredom till dinnertime. The oriental carpet was worn through to the woven hemp in a rectangle the size of a coffin. The only pile and print left were in the middle where the coffins had stood, one after the other, in a procession through time and the family tree.

Amy walked first to the mantle and stared silently at a pair of china bobblehead dogs, of which no one remembered the history. Next, she crawled over the divan and sat behind it on the floor in the corner, which occupied a few minutes and was entertaining because it was forbidden. Climbing back out, she found a pack of Beemans Pepsin Gum on the windowsill and helped herself to a very hard stick. While she chewed, she turned and faced the other corner.

Looming there at an angle was a large dark upright piano. It had been bought at Sears and had been drawn up the hollow by horse and wagon and had never been tuned since it was installed in 1894.

Amy's long empty afternoons were filled with rituals, one of which was to examine the piano, the bench, and its contents. These items never changed or moved from visit to visit or year to year. Part of the magic was opening the bench and finding the World War I medals and the corncob pipe exactly where she had found them at the time of the last visit. It was instinctively understood that they had lain there untouched for decades and would remain so forever. There was a funny greeting card with a rooster on it, signed by "Aunt Mae, 1917" addressed to Orie, buried under dry old sheet music that had a buttery feel and would crumble if you picked it up.

After closing the piano bench, the next step was to sit down and play a few hideous clanging notes, which came spiraling out of the huge wooden machine and tauntingly resembled music. The ivory keys were yellow and had a coating of gritty black coal dust. Amy's fingertips were cold and had small black circles of dust on them when she finally gave up with a sigh. She could not wring a song out of the piano, so she propped the top open by standing on the bench and peered inside. She saw a Beemans pepsin gum wrapper, some green stamps, and a white hairpin left from some long-ago session in which

Great-Grandma had valiantly retrieved her most ambitious piece of music from her unrehearsed memory.

This archeological treasure was covered by a few dried poinsettia leaves and a gentle blanket of thick dust, which year after silent year had made its way into the unplayed piano. It was now used only to hold Christmas cards and an oil lamp for a brief period of glory each season. Decades ago, a visitor might have tried to lure out a few carols, but finding the piano so out of tune, soon became discouraged and embarrassed and would give up and wander off to the kitchen and the coal stove instead.

Sufficiently chilled and having exhausted all the entertainment value out of the parlor, Amy now left the room by climbing out of the window next to the piano, which let into the back kitchen pantry. She loved to appear in the kitchen from the pantry, imagining that the grown-ups were mystified by this. Back in the warm kitchen, she leaned against Orie's chair and traced the design in the carved wooden back with her finger.

The Tablecloth, 1926

Clark Minor Covert was dead. His widow, Anna Priscilla, lived a lonely life in a mountain hollow in Westmoreland County on a bend in the Youghiogheny River.

Anna had left Allegheny City to return to her childhood home, now owned by her sister. They took in boarders and had rooms and outbuildings, which they let out to miners, for whom she cooked, baked, and washed. Her brood of brothers and uncles did the man chores, but they also made her hard life harder. Only her old-maid sister Sarah Jane helped to boil the mountains of linens and empty the cinders and ashes from the coal stove. Anna's daughter Orie worked in McKeesport, earning enough to provide money for coal, and dry goods.

They lived just the way their parents had, feeding and housing a stream of humanity that through the years had included the last of the Indians from the hollow, Civil War veterans, railroad men, and eventually the coal miners. Together they gardened by hand the four acres that fed them and the miners year-round.

Somehow, they found time and energy late at night to crochet. Anna had just finished a huge tablecloth in linen thread so fine, she could hardly see it by the kerosene lantern. It was strong, though, and when she showed it to her granddaughter Ruthie one Sunday, Sarah Jane, sitting in the rocker near the coal stove, quietly remarked that "I hope you like it. You'll probably be washing it for a hundred years."

For Ruthie, being there with the old women was like going to heaven. These old mysterious people loved her in a way that her mother did not.

"Teach me how to crochet please, Granny," Ruth said.

"We'll get Orie to teach you. She's the seamstress."

Orie did teach Ruthie to crochet. And eventually, the tablecloth would belong to Ruth, and it still comes out on special days on Amy's table.

The Back Stairway, 1961

Crawling over shoes, leather books, and a jumble of unfamiliar tools and household items was the only way to navigate what Amy suddenly realized was a narrow stairway. At first, she had regarded the steps as an odd sort of shelving because she had never seen anyone use them to ascend to the second story of the house or descend.

She had discovered this mysterious storage place while exploring the master bedroom. The long mantelpiece held two ancient pistols, which she knew she mustn't touch, even if they had not been out of reach. A bed, far too high for her to climb up on, commanded the austere room. Each window had a roller-blind. After grabbing the handmade pull and running one up and down till her arm got tired, she played with the other one until it coiled itself angrily in the top of the window. She stood in the middle of the room and regarded the wash-stand. A white pitcher and basin had recent splash marks around them. Poking around in the droplets, she made tiny trails in the fine black coal dust that pervaded the entire house. A tilted wavy Amy watched her from the beveled mirror.

Across the room was a narrow door. The hair on the back of her neck rose as she opened it. A riot of smells rose up from an unlit narrow space. The aromas of stale leather, sweat, old cooking odors, and of course, cigarette and coal smoke slipped out like released prisoners. Quietly, she tiptoed down into this odd place, going deeper and deeper into the chilly dark.

There was a door at the bottom, which she studied carefully. It was fixed on the inside with a black wrought iron bolt. The paint was creamy yellow, the color of corn bread. Suddenly, she turned around, clambered quickly back to the top, popped out through the tiny door into the master bedroom, and ran into the hall, down the main staircase, swung around the newel post in the front hall, and tore into the kitchen.

The grown-ups' conversation paused almost imperceptibly and then resumed when she didn't interrupt. Her habit was to burst into a room talking, and she was accustomed to becoming the center of attention, especially if her mother was in the room. (This would induce in her a lifelong habit of interrupting people, which she combated with varying degrees of success.)

On this occasion, she was preoccupied with her research and stood quietly in the kitchen doorway and studied a narrow door behind Aunt Orie's chair. It was gray, like all the woodwork in the kitchen, and it was the exact dimension as the yellow door inside the little staircase. She ran out of the kitchen and back upstairs to the master bedroom and tiptoed down the miniature steps again. Seated atop a pair of high leather boots with hooks and eyes and which smelled like manure, she pressed her ear to the door.

Aunt Orie was laughing…just on the other side of the door! As Amy listened, she realized they were talking about her! Reaching up, she pulled the dark bolt. After it resisted a little, it clacked open. The door opened only a few inches then banged against the back of Aunt Orie's high-backed chair. The warm smoky air from the kitchen flowed over her face, and she realized that it was cold in the stairway.

She pressed her face in the opening and tried to poke her head out and proclaim her great discovery!

She waited and heard two words. "Close it." Orie gave commands matter-of-factly.

No one ever argued or disobeyed her. Amy pulled the door shut and closed the bolt. She heard them all laughing as she ran up the stairs. She was disappointed that the secret stairs were no secret.

CHAPTER 5

Bernie and Ruth

Bernie

Ruth

My father and mother were born in 1920 and 1921, respectively. True children of the Great Depression, they had stories to tell that were sad, funny, and inspiring. They both were artists and loved music. He was the middle child of eleven, and she was an only child. Although in character very similar, they had personalities that were opposites. She was wild and eccentric; he was solid, strict, and reliable.

My adulthood was well underway before I realized that they balanced each other perfectly, using humor, patience, and respect to do so. They had a tiny private world from which they viewed the universe around them. My brother and I were welcome citizens of their world, and it formed our values and personalities. We felt that our family was a little out of the ordinary but special because of it.

"People are allowed to be different from each other," Dad told me. "Every town seems to have a few characters, or a recluse, or people who have special needs. They deserve respect and any help you can give them." He expected Bob and me to protect those weaker than ourselves. He told us to "love the unlovely."

He did not believe in animals in the house, but because he loved my mother, we had a profusion of pets and domestic animals that served no purpose, except to create cost and work for him. He was kind to them all and could be heard muttering soft words to them of complaint and comfort as he fed them, built fences, mended sheds, and eventually was responsible for their peaceful deaths and burials. "There you go, you poor miserable fellow creature," he would say, quoting *Great Expectations*.

My mother was a rainbow of emotions and ideas, afraid of almost everything and totally fearless. She did not know how many dollars were in a dime, and was wildly generous. She was a strong comforter and advocate as a mother, but she herself was still totally a child. She read everything and had a vivid imagination. She had many talents and a slender grasp of reality that my father found amusing and endearing and which he battled to the best of his ability.

Aunt Jane's Rescue, 1948

Bernie was sure he loved Ruth, and so it was time for him to meet her family. He was a little uncomfortable because she was polished and well read, and he felt like a country boy. She was very intelligent, kind, and funny. She said her family were "hillbillies." He wasn't sure if he believed her. She said she was part Indian, and he did believe that because she had huge dark brown eyes that were almost black, and also, he wanted to believe her.

This morning, they had driven deep into the Youghiogheny River Valley and deeper still into an old coal mining hollow. He was enchanted when they came through the narrow track, crossed over a rushing creek, and pulled up in front of a very large house that bore a century of poverty and loving neglect proudly. It was a T-shaped wooden farm house, paint long gone, weathered to gray.

The lush dew-covered grass was ankle-deep and had been gently and evenly coiffed by Ruth's uncle Tom with a two-wheel manual mower. Along the uphill side of the long yard was an amazing dry stone wall, waist-high, atop which a riot of roses, pink and pinker, gave a fragrance that would define "rose." The tumbling wave of flowers and huge ferns drew the eye in a sweeping line toward the house.

It was nestled against a steep side of the hollow, adorned with many porches. Each porch had turned wooden pillars that made one think of a scene from a Western movie. There was no indoor plumbing. There was an outhouse in back. His eyes climbed up the looming forested hill behind the house, and halfway up the sheer, he saw a little path enter the shadow of the trees.

"Where does that go?" he asked Ruth.

"Into our coal shaft," she said and grinned.

He giggled. He was amused, either because it was true, or because it wasn't.

They came into the kitchen, and Bernie shook hands with Aunt Jane and her sister Anna, Ruth's grandma. He met Ruth's parents, Bob and Betty, and Bob's siblings, the infamous Tom and the inscrutable Aunt Orie. Their brother Bill was not there. He had moved to Michigan to live on a reservation, which was a source of deep shame to his family.

Bernie was charmed by the big house and was entertained by meeting them all. They fulfilled every characterization Ruth had given, including the one of "hillbilly."

In the kitchen, the aroma of roast beef, green beans, and corn bread blended with the ever-familiar odor of coal smoke. The potatoes were "bilin'" on top of the black stove that dominated the house and had been there since it was built and upon which the women cooked summer and winter.

The round oak claw-foot table in the kitchen was too small for this large company, so in the next room, the dining table was set for ten. Ruth's favorite cousin Bert was there with his fiancée, May, who was also meeting the family for the first time that day.

The double-pedestal dining table in the next room could seat twelve. Towering against one side wall was a breakfront with curved glass doors. Along the other wall was a matching sideboard covered with serving dishes. T-back oak chairs surrounded the table. These things were very old and much finer than Bernie had expected. The table was set with china all around, and in the center was a plate with a huge ball of fresh butter and a glass bowl of Grandma's chili sauce, which they pronounced "chill-a-sauce." It was gleaming and dark red, the last treasures of the summer garden. The green beans in the casserole had been picked that morning, as had the late onions, which were crispy and browned in butter.

When they were all seated at the table, there was a lot of chatter and laughter. They seemed like happy people, Bernie thought. Even the sinister Tom made jokes and laughed at times. Like everyone else in those days, their conversation was speckled with references to "The War." At every meal someone remembered a story about rationing. Friends lost in battle were remembered, and tales of joyous homecomings were retold. Bob and Tom were telling the story of encountering each other in France during World War I, for if you talked about the recent war, they had to remind you about their war—"The Big One."

Bob had been in a guardhouse outside of Verdun. A tall soldier strolled past with a helmet down over his eyes and a cigarette in his mouth. A moment later, he strolled past the little window going the other direction. Then for a third time, he strolled by. Bob called out, "Hey, you there! Do you want something?"

The soldier turned and grinned a huge toothy grin. To Bob's amazement, it was the yellow grin of his brother Tom. They had not heard from each other since they had joined the army.

Everyone at the table was laughing uproariously even though they had all, except Bernie and May, heard the story many times before. Bernie lifted his coffee cup to take a sip. As he did, Ruth screamed, "Look at Aunt Jane!"

Over the rim of his cup, he looked at the old lady. Her white hair was pinned neatly in a bun; she wore a prim dark blue dress with long sleeves ruffled at the wrist and a handmade lace apron. You could see her gold watch chain dropping behind the bib of it. Her face was dark purple, and tears were streaming down her cheeks.

"She's choking!" yelled Bert. Antique chairs tipped over as Bob and Tom dove at her. Aunt Jane was snatched from her chair. Bernie was paralyzed. More quickly than he could take it in, the two middle-aged men turned her upside down.

Now revealed were lace petticoats and undergarments that had been out of vogue for fifty years. They held her aloft by slender black-stockinged ankles and, to his astonishment, shook her. With a terrific hacking noise, she produced a large barely chewed select morsel of roast beef.

Her nephews placed her back in her chair. She smoothed her apron, straightened her gold chain, and daintily rescued the gold watch, which was now nestled atop her head and skewered with a white hair pin. She dropped it neatly behind her apron. As she patted her hair back into place, Bernie set his coffee cup back down into the saucer in his other hand. *Click.*

Dinner and conversation resumed undeterred. He and May looked at each other. Both were meeting this family for the first time and wondered what the future would have in store for them if they joined their ranks.

The Trolley to Harmony, 1928

Grandpa Jake and Ruthie got on the trolley in Pittsburgh and after one transfer were on the Harmony short line, northbound for the town of Harmony. Ruthie was excited because these picnic outings alone with her Grandpa were the highlight of her life. He wasn't like her mother, Elizabeth, who was given to fits of rage or coldness when she didn't speak at all, and he was different from Ruthie's father who was indifferent and, well, rather stupid and terrified of his wife.

No, Jake was different from everyone in the world, it seemed to her. He was very, very old, perhaps fifty or sixty. He was born in Switzerland during the American Civil War. She didn't know that explained his peculiarly expressive blend of English, French, and German. Later on in life, she would realize a linguistic capacity, which she would credit to her conversations with Jake. He wasn't afraid of his wife, Grandma Jake. Her real name was Elizabeth—Elizabeth

Kemmer. She became a Muehlethaler when she married Jake when she was fifteen. He was very kind to her. He had to watch her closely, though, because she couldn't seem to grasp some of life's basic rules. One day, he came home from his workday as a boilermaker tired, coal blackened, and hungry to find her holding a little black baby.

"Vat is this?" he cried.

"I got a baby!" she told him joyfully.

"But mein Lizzy, from vere did you get it?"

"At the store. It was in a buggy. It was so sweet I took it!"

The frantic colored woman was weeping when he brought the baby back to the store down the street. He was glad it was not a white child, then there would have been police, and his English was not perfect...

As Ruthie and Jake rode the trolley they were quiet. He was rather deaf, and the bumping of the wheels and the mixed voices of the other passengers made it difficult for him to hear her. She didn't mind; she loved to look out the window and daydream as she watched the 1920s Pennsylvania countryside slide past. The supreme moment for her was when a certain vista came into view. Each time they made this journey to Harmony and came through the little hamlet of Wexford and jogged into the next sweeping valley, she held her breath as she glimpsed a white house on a hill. In her mind, it was "The House."

Ruthie imagined what it would be like to live in that house. It was tall and plain yet very friendly looking. Perched on a knob, it overlooked a panorama. There were no neighbors, no cars, no sidewalks, just acres and acres of grass and corn and some cows. The broad front steps up to the added-on Victorian porch were very different from the stoop of her Northside row house, and she felt sure there were no rules against sitting on them or playing outside. The horses she saw probably lived there and were happier than the iceman's horse. She made a promise to herself that someday, she would live in a house like that.

*****

Jake helped her down the trolley steps, and they found themselves on a wooden platform. The whole town of Harmony looked like a picnic—colorful houses decorated with gingerbread and the square laid out straight and perfect like a tablecloth. It didn't seem bunched-up and twisted like so many streets in Pittsburgh. The Harmony Inn dominated the town square. However, they would not visit the inn today. They had their own picnic lunch basket and intended to pick berries. They walked just a few blocks and the town ended abruptly, becoming a field full of "pick your own" berry plants. An old man collected five cents from Jake and waved them into the field.

To Ruthie, everything her grandfather did was wonderful. She loved picking the berries. He would stop while filling a tin and say, "The most of them are for your Mutti, but this one, he is so special, you must eat him now." With her mouth full of luscious strawberry, she gazed up at him and decided then and there that berries must have something to do with love.

Papa Rick, 1931

The sun was blazing. Papa Rick didn't bathe much, and Bernie could smell him even when he was at the far end of a row. It was all right, though; this is why Bernie had him and the hilltop all to himself. No one else wanted to learn how to grow strawberries. He had ten brothers and sisters (counting baby Richard, who had died during the flu epidemic). They all sure would want to eat the berries, though.

The houses of the town of Jeannette far below looked tiny and skinny, stripey and side-by-side, with steep yards like ribbons, a chicken coop and outhouse at the end of each stripe of green. The May breeze was brisk up here, and the old-man smell blew away. The clean weed and dirt and worm smell warmed up around your face when you bent over to work.

There was a satisfying gritty chunking sound each time Papa Rick sunk his hoe. Each strawberry plant had to be cultivated by hand, and the runners set; you had to place a little rock on each offspring plant's lifeline till it rooted. On the other side of the knob were the plants they had pulled all the blossoms off to make them strong for next year's berries, and the best front patch was covered with the white unripe fruit that they would be picking when ruby red in June.

Papa Rick didn't say much. He came from two types of quiet people—the English and the Seneca. Even though he was only eleven, Bernie liked the conversationless quiet. It was always noisy at home—thirteen people in a two-bedroom row house, and now during the Depression, two of his aunts came to eat every night. They had to sit on the radiator behind the girl's side of the table and hold their plates. Aunt Margaret smelled pretty bad when the radiator got hot, and it was fun to watch his sisters make faces and roll their eyes. Dinner was fun in general. Somehow they found a reason to laugh, and he tried to eat as slowly as he could to make his one helping last.

He realized that he had been standing and gazing down on the town for a long time and brought himself back to the task at hand, setting runners. Only about 150 more plants to go. They had room for about six hundred plants. That was enough for the family to eat fresh berries every day for two to three weeks and have jam for winter too. That is, of course, if no late frost stole them, and there was just enough rain and not too much, which would rot them, and the birds didn't eat more than their share.

Now if you could put in about five or ten thousand plants, he thought, *you wouldn't have to worry about the birds*. Why, you'd have enough to sell! *Imagine…a whole strawberry farm. A fellow would need a tractor to manage that!* He loved tractors! Bernie dreamed about tractors while he worked. Then he heard the unmistakable thrilling sound of an airplane. His eyes darted down to watch all the people pour out of the houses and shops to look for it, but he tore his gaze away so he wouldn't miss one second of the flight of the plane right over their heads. He forgot about tractors as he tried to imagine himself up in an airplane.

A Soldier's Dilemma, 1942

When Bernie got on the bus in Pensacola, there was just one empty seat. It was in the last row in the white section next to a small thin young soldier, whose destination was the same as his. They had finished basic training in Florida and were on their way to Texas for flight training in the Army Air Corps.

It was hot on the bus. Bernie grew sleepy. He daydreamed and wondered if it was hot at home in Pittsburgh. He felt the bus stop and after only a moment, start to move again. He opened his eyes and watched a pretty young colored woman with a toddler come down the aisle. She was expecting soon and struggled with a heavy bag.

The colored section behind him was full, even the aisle was filled to the line painted on the floor. She was forced to stand next to Bernie's seat in the white section of the aisle. There were at least a hundred miles to go to the next stop. He rose. He was tall and thin and wore his Army Air Corps uniform handsomely. "Here, have a seat," he said. The bus grew quiet. All conversation stopped.

The young woman whispered, "Oh, no, suh, thank you." She looked down. There had been a flicker of fear in her eyes as she spoke.

He hesitated and then sat back down. Conversations resumed slowly. She swayed gently as the bus rolled along the highway. Drops of perspiration stood neatly on her arm, which was inches from his face. He was deeply troubled. Time went by, and miles went by. She clutched the seat nervously to keep from falling. Perspiration now rolled down her arm and trickled onto the small hand of her child. Bernie grew more and more distressed as she stood there, and then he shook his head as the tired little boy sank down into the dust and cigarette butts on the floor and leaned his face against his mother's trembling leg.

He reached down and pulled the small child up into his lap. The young man in the seat beside him said, "Hey! What the hell do you think you are doin' with that nigger?" He pronounced it "Hay-ell," like a curse word, not the name of a place. It was as though he needed two syllables to hold all his hate.

Once again, it grew very quiet in the bus. Everyone, white and black, waited to see what would happen. Bernie sighed and handed the child back to his mother. Then he unfolded himself into a tower above the other soldier. He turned slowly and leaned over him. His fine high forehead gleamed, and his face was so red that his blond eyebrows stood out white. Unwavering blue eyes pinned the insolent soldier in his seat. Bernie's gaze revealed a moral confidence that made the other man look away.

After a moment, Bernie turned back to the young mother and offered his seat to her again. "Thank you, please no, suh. It's against the law."

He reluctantly sat down and reached for the tired child and tenderly lifted him into his lap again. This time, no one spoke. Everyone rode in silence in the unmoving heat. He suffered along with the woman standing in the aisle, and the little boy slept.

Bert Gets Even, 1947

Twenty-six years old and still single. Ruth was pretty, slender, funny. Everyone loved her, especially her cousin Bert. But her parents were cruel, and she had no brothers or sisters, so when things in life went wrong, she turned to Bert for companionship and consolation.

She had dated a lot of men, mostly soldiers. One relationship had been serious, but she lost him in the war. Now, here she was, single, not really young, working at Wallek's book store in the Jenkins Arcade building in Pittsburgh. Not many prospects, she thought.

"You know, Ruthie, there are a lot of guys your age going to school on the GI Bill, just like me," Bert said. "I could introduce you to some of them."

He attended the Art Institute of Pittsburgh on Fort Duquesne Boulevard, a six-minute walk to Jenkins Arcade. "These are interesting, talented guys. I could send them over for lunch dates with you. You never know! It could work out!"

She sighed as she put on her lipstick and prepared for one last blind date with one of "Bert's Artists." She had agreed to these serial blind dates, and even though Bert sent some of his favorite acquaintances over, she had to tell him each time, "Well, I just don't like him."

Bert was getting frustrated—in fact, annoyed. Just what did she want?

He had an idea. He would get her to agree to just one more date. There was this one fellow, Bernie, who was a nice enough fellow, and he was very talented. But he was a hick, and shy, and poor, and a bad dresser. Bert couldn't figure him out. He wasn't like a lot of the other artists—slick and ambitious, trying to be like that up-and-coming Carnegie Mellon University student Andy Warhol. Bernie was conservative, kind of backward. Bert figured that Ruth would really dislike him. *This will fix her. She doesn't think any of my friends are good enough for her. Well, I'll get even. Today for lunch, she gets Bernie Stern.*

She stood behind the front desk, surrounded by stacks of books, and waited for what she called "Bert's Disappointment Du Jour" to arrive.

At 12:15, the door opened, and in the doorway stood her blind date. Smiling at her was a tall, thin man wearing a worn leather flight jacket, Sears work pants, no tie, and no hat. He needed a haircut. He had a big nose and big ears. He looked at her for a moment and said, "Gloriosky, Zero, you make me feel glad all over!"

She couldn't believe it! He was quoting the funny papers. He must read The Daily Cat Doodle by Jean Tuttle, which she loved! Zero was the name of Little Annie Rooney's dog, who sprang to life around the time of the Little Orphan Annie craze.

She looked at him and started to laugh. They headed out for lunch, and they laughed the whole time. The minutes flew too quickly. They parted on the sidewalk, and she watched him run off down the street. He stopped and yelled back to her, "I'll get your number from Bert!"

She was laughing and curb walking (one foot on the curb, the other in the street, up down, up down, arms wide out) as she went back to work. Her coworker Lorraine was standing in front of Jenkins Arcade watching her. "What are you so happy about?" she asked.

"I'm going to marry Bernie Stern," she crowed.

The Jenkins Arcade building was seven stories tall, a giant when it was built in 1910. It housed 215 shops and businesses ranging from dentists and opticians to button makers and bookstores. It was torn down amidst controversy in 1982 to make room for Fifth Avenue Place.

One defender of preserving the building as an historical landmark said this: "[The Arcade's] high ornate ceiling, multiplicity of shops, and inviting warmth will be replaced by another stark, unimaginative edifice devoid of character."

Another said, "It's a little city all its own."

For seventy-two years, real stories like my parent's first date happened in that "little city."

In the Workshop, 1977

The mellow wood was silky smooth, and Bernie ran his fingers through the fine wood dust. He was sanding the soundboard of a 1918 Steinway piano that he was rebuilding with his daughter. She was a piano tuner—in fact, a rebuilder. His friends and acquaintances couldn't believe it when he had let Amy go to piano tuning school instead of college, but he had known it was right for her.

When she wanted to start to rebuild pianos, he finished a large room in the basement of The House for her workshop and built her some workbenches. Now just a few years later, she was a success and needed to hire help. He was the first to apply. *Pittsburgh Magazine* had just done an article entitled "Daughter Knows Best" about the piano shop and her thriving business. The article told how Amy was training him to rebuild pianos with her, giving them new lives.

He had retired early from the telephone company to care for his ailing wife. Her struggle was going to be long, and so was his. Always an active man, it was hard to sit, never far from her side, waiting for her to need him. He had made a lovely place for the hospital bed in the bay window of the living room. She could look out at the fields and see anyone who came up the driveway.

So as his wife slept, he worked in the piano shop. He had run a phone line to the shop so she could call him when he was needed. He could field calls for Amy's business when she was out on the road tuning pianos.

He mused as he worked. His life had been so full of changes and surprises. As a child he had dreamed of being an artist, or a berry farmer, or an airplane pilot. During the depression, he had worked in a toy makers shop, then at the Jeannette Glass Factory. He had been a house painter and had gone to refrigeration school all before joining the Army Air Corps when Pearl Harbor was attacked. He and three of his brothers signed up the same day.

After the war, he went to the Art Institute of Pittsburgh on the GI Bill. There he met Bert, who introduced Bernie to his favorite cousin Ruth, whom Bernie married in 1948. He took a job with the phone company when Bobby came along in '49. He planted acres and acres of strawberries and kept up his artwork. He always said that his job at the phone company financed his painting and his strawberry habit.

Now here he was, starting a new career again, rebuilding fine old grand pianos. It was exacting but rewarding work. Amy held to high standards and had a booming business and a great reputation. But how could anyone have guessed he would be doing this? His daughter had taught him how to string pianos, restore keyboards, and how to repair cracked soundboards. As he worked, his mind drifted back to the first time he had ever heard or seen a piano.

A Boy's First Music, 1932

As the horse-drawn wagon rumbled slowly up 2nd Street, a small group of barefoot boys formed to watch. Trailing behind it, they scrutinized the huge rectangular object in the wagon. It was wrapped in blankets, and it emitted mysterious clanging sounds as the cart wheels jostled over the cobblestones. The boys were not the only curious spectators. People from up and down the street gathered on the sidewalk to watch the first piano in the neighborhood being delivered.

It was a small German Catholic ghetto. A few families had radios, but most did not. Bernie's family went to church every Sunday, but the pipe organ had not worked for years. So other than the priest singing the mass and the congregational singing, the only music Bernie ever heard was the toneless rendition of the national anthem his sixth grade droned each school day morning.

Men with forearms like hams were unloading the monstrous machine. They put one end down on the street and balanced it on that end while the driver skillfully pulled the cart out from under the piano. Grunting, they lowered it down to the street, and at the last second, one of the men kicked a flat dolly under it. As they rolled it along the sidewalk toward the front door, the small crowd parted like the Red Sea. The men stuffed the big piano through the door, and as many neighbors as could fit flowed into the house behind them. The rest stood around on the porch.

Bernie was tall, thin, quick, and smart. He ran around to the side of the house and squirmed behind a bush right under a window of the room receiving the piano—the parlor. The newly pruned bush scratched him and poked him in the ribs. On tiptoes, he peered in and watched the piano movers tilt the piano up and pull out the dolly and set the piano down. They removed the straps and blankets and then pushed the gleaming instrument into the corner.

"Make way," they muttered as they carried the equipment out of the house. The happy new owner thanked them, shook their hands, and then turned to regard the piano. She clasped her hands under her chin for a moment then sat down to touch the ivory keys for the first time. Everyone got quiet.

Her cheeks were flushed, and her hands were trembling. Even though she had no sheet music, her hands moved over the keys with growing confidence. Beautiful melodies began to pour out of the piano. To Bernie, it seemed as though the music rolled across the room and out of the window directly to him alone. Such sounds, so alive and personal! Booming bass tones and sparkling treble notes came out of the piano in waves.

Fifty years later, as he ran his hands over the finished sound-board, he found himself reliving this memory. He was surrounded by pianos in different stages of repair. Some were getting restrung, some new keys and hammers, some being completely restored. Together, he and Amy would rebuild pianos, many old enough to be the very one which played the first piano music he ever heard.

CHAPTER 6

Life Is a Process

Life Is a Process

Life is a process of moving from one joy to the next, I believe. Perhaps this is the difference between an optimist and a pessimist. An optimist sees life as a series of good things, punctuated by difficulties, while a pessimist sees life as a series of miseries interrupted occasionally by brief periods of relief. An optimist living the grateful life inevitably leads to one pessimist or another accusing him of having better luck.

I choose the more helpful view. I move from the goodbye kiss of a loved one to a moment of joy in the garden, to wholesome employment that I am grateful for, like stepping stones in a turbulent stream. The torrent that rages in between them is made up of the broken furnace, the encounter with inevitable age in the mirror, aches and pains, a diagnosis I don't wish to hear, bills due yesterday. But I try to never let those interfere with the flow of faith, hope, and joy in my life.

Of course, it is more difficult at times. The stepping stones of joy are hardest to find when the interruption is a divorce, a sick child, cancer, or death. Nonetheless, I maintain that all of these things, which happen to us all, are more manageable, more valuable, more enriching when viewed with head held high and eyes on the Master. Thus far, I have had sufficient blessings and strength to carry on, to the great irritation of the pessimists in my life.

Sock Skating, 1966

Amy had the good side of the wall. Well, it wasn't really a wall; it was a partition made of lumber and drywall scraps that Bernie had around, thrown together quickly in the biggest bedroom in The House, which was above the kitchen. It divided the room exactly in half, and Amy and Bobby each had a twin bed on their respective sides.

Amy's side had the studs and bracing, which made delightful little shelves to hold all the tiny trinkets little girls love. Troll dolls, rings, stuffed animals, a cologne bottle, a sachet—she made the most of the new arrangement. She curled up in her new space and gazed at her "display" as she fell asleep to the sound of coughing.

Bernie and Ruth had moved out of that room and set up their double bed in the smallest room. Finally, in the third bedroom were two more twin beds, set up for Aunt Orie and Uncle Tom.

Tom was sick, very sick. Bernie had taken time off work and brought them in from Guffy Hollow this morning. Ruth was tending to Tom. Always a thin man, now he was thinner than ever. And the coughing never stopped. Ruth didn't know for sure, but she suspected it was lung cancer. They were making arrangements to take him to the Veterans Hospital in a few days for tests if he didn't improve. Amy loved the hubbub, the changes, the company, and sharing a room with her big brother!

In the morning, they all had breakfast together before school. By the time Amy walked to the bus stop, rode the bus, arrived at the school, and got into her seat in the fourth-grade room, she forgot all about what was going on at home. By the next day, she was used to having more people in the house and at the table.

A few days later, she was walking home from the bus, looking up at The House, thinking about how kind and generous her parents were, taking care of a sick relative they didn't even like very much. She walked along Harmony Road and cut up into the field through a plot of crab apple trees. There were almost as many bees as blossoms. It was a beautiful day in late May. In the worn pathway, she was surrounded by pale green sunlight, dimmed and colored by young leaves. The sky was blue between the pink and green branches. She could feel the edge of the little orchard, like a golden wall. In front of her was the sunlit expanse that rolled up to the driveway, then up to The House. Amy lingered to pick some violets that had popped up between the rows of strawberry plants as she came through the front field.

She stepped up onto the driveway and looked around. Her father's car was in the driveway. Why would he be home from work so early? She ran toward The House. A strange combination of smells was coming from the kitchen. It smelled like Mum was making roast beef, but the aroma was mixed with the smell of smoke and…bleach.

As she came up the sidewalk, she saw a sight even stranger than the smell. There was a fire going twenty feet from the kitchen door. Bernie came out of the house with an armful of curtains and pillows and threw them on the blaze. He was frowning until he saw her. Then he broke into a smile. She knew to stay away from him and the fire. She choked on the dense smoke and looked at the fire again. There was a mattress burning and the remnants of their living room couch!

In the kitchen, Ruth stood watching the contents of the large canner come to a boil. It was full of dinner dishes and glasses! Sheets reeking of bleach hung out on the backyard clothesline in the sunshine.

Confused, Amy sat down in the nearest chair. Her mother had a worried look on her face, but when she turned and saw Amy, she lit up with a big smile.

"Isn't this something, honey? We are going to have the cleanest house around!"

"Why is Daddy burning a mattress and all that stuff? Where is Aunt Orie? What are you doing?"

"Aunt Orie is with Uncle Tom at the hospital. It turns out he is really sick. He has something called Tuberculosis."

Still confused, Amy just looked at her.

"The doctors asked Daddy and me to boil everything we all touch and to burn what couldn't be boiled or bleached. Look at how clean the house is! And your toys were all washed and are outside!" Ruth made this all sound like something good and wonderful.

Amy got up and looked in the living room and the playroom (what they called the den). Empty. Floors, spotless from scrubbing, smelled like bleach.

Ruth stood beside her and put her arm around her. "This is what people do to keep from getting sick too, honey. There is nothing to worry about. It is just what we do."

Amy looked at her. She was smiling. And now she had the big Johnson's Baby Powder can in her hand. "What is that for?" Amy asked.

Ruth replied, "I have a great idea. Take your shoes off. Keep your socks on. We are going to sock skate!"

They shrieked with laughter and sprinkled the powder on the floor of all three empty rooms. They skidded around in circles, faster and faster, chasing, sometimes falling. Out of breath, white powder on their hands and knees and bottoms, they paused for a minute to rest. Bernie was leaning in the doorway grinning and looking at them. After a minute, he took his shoes off too and yelled, "Look out! I'm gonna get you!" and joined in the game.

They sock skated off and on for a few days. Eventually, new furniture came, piece by piece. Orie stayed near the hospital for a while and eventually went back to Guffy. Amy never saw Uncle Tom again.

They all waited for days to see if they got red marks where the doctor had stamped a little needle-pronged tester in their arms. Her father said God would protect them. Amy was the only one who got a red lump on her arm. She had a real blood test a few days later. Her mother cried with relief when they got the results: exposed, noninfected. School had ended for the year, but she could go to fifth grade in the fall!

The bedrooms were put back to normal, except there were no curtains, and Amy had learned a few really important lessons. She had learned that things are only things and can be replaced or done without. She learned that even when situations seem terribly grave, you can still laugh and have fun. She learned that people take care of each other no matter what. And most of all, she learned that God is always with you.

December 20, 1981, 12:05 a.m. It's Still Christmas

"It's over," Bernie said softly to his daughter and then hung up the phone. She dashed out the door of her little cottage, nestled next to The House she had grown up in. Snow burned her bare feet as she ran across the yard between the two homes up a little slope to The House. Amy came in the back door to find him sitting at the claw-foot kitchen table, staring into an empty coffee cup. He had sat at this table with Ruth when it was still in Guffy, and he had placed many meals upon it with her after it had come here to The House. Amy sat down and looked at him.

"She stopped breathing." After a tender pause, he looked down at her feet. "Put some shoes on."

She stuffed her feet into a pair of her father's socks without taking her eyes off him. His face was gray. After years of dreading this moment, it was here and it seemed unreal. It was also a relief. Bernie, Amy, and Bob were all tired from watching Ruth struggle to stay cheerful, to eat, finally to breathe. Now there would be no more struggle.

There was nothing to do till morning. Bernie went to bed. Amy curled up on her mother's hospital bed nestled in the bay window, and she dozed off watching for the headlight beams of her brother's car to swing through the late December bare trees that lined the driveway.

That broad old window faces northeast. It was not headlights, but the slanting rays of sunrise that awakened her. She opened her eyes without moving and saw Bob sleeping on the couch across the room. He was still dressed, in fact, still wearing his coat, his hands tucked under his arms. He is a long man, and his feet, shoes still on, hung over the end of the couch. She didn't make a sound, but he felt her wake up and opened his eyes. A tear ran from the corner of his eye, and he just murmured, "I know."

The funeral preparations were made amidst the carnival of Christmas. The season refused to pause to acknowledge their sorrow. Jolly Christmas music became imbued with a secret melancholy, but deep inside this melancholy was a quiet joy for Amy.

Just two days earlier, while mother and daughter were alone, Ruth had confided to Amy that she felt like a ship that had crossed the stormy ocean, full of treasure. She said she did not want to sink in the harbor. She asked Amy if she thought that the Savior would accept her at this last desperate moment. Amy assured her that He

114

was waiting for her with open arms, that her long illness and suffering were a courtship in which He had wooed her.

They prayed together for the first time since Amy was a child. It would be the last time. Ruth lay on her pillow, and breathing very shallowly, said she would be in heaven this Christmas. So, amid the sorrow, there is joy.

It was a few days till Christmas, but instead of shopping, the time was spent at the funeral home. At the end of the long evening of greeting family and friends, the little family of three headed home. Silent in the car, Bob drove very, very slowly up the old driveway in the dark. As if to give comfort, the road rocked them gently. Bernie was looking tired. As they crested the hill, they were astonished to see a Christmas tree glowing in the bay window right where Ruth and Bernie had always put one.

They came into the house to find Bob's friend Larry. He stood smiling silently with his hands in his pockets. While they were out doing their sad duty, he had replaced hospital bed and oxygen tanks with a lovely tree, hastily adorned with only lights. Deeply touched, they did not speak. He looked at them and shrugged shyly. "It's still Christmas," he said.

Today

I am still here, in The House. Being here has become a part of my identity. We all know a house is just a thing. I believe that. But after a long period of time, a thing can take on a persona, and I have to be careful not to love her too much.

The House stands resolute in time. Her nineteenth-century square nails still hold her tight. Her cellar's dusty dirt floors sleep peacefully under a blanket of concrete. Her windows are the eyes of a wise old woman, gazing tenderly down at her green skirts embroidered with flowers, tomatoes, and of course, berries.

As the town around us develops, wildlife is crowded onto our refuge, and we welcome them. As long as I am here, I will treasure The House and her land, with its trails and troubles, its fruits, and its creatures. I hope someone will follow me and keep her. I hope they will thank God daily for her five little acres of unpolluted land and the comfort and sustenance they give.

"Christmas, Present"
Lois Duncan

I saw the Ghost-of-Christmas Past
Glide by our lighted tree.
Her arms were filled with dolls and toys,
And all were meant for me.

I sensed the rustle of her skirts.
Her blouse was trimmed with lace,
And when she turned to smile at me
She wore my mother's face.

Just as the vision slipped from sight,
I heard my daughter call.
Wild footsteps clattered on the stair;
Shrill giggles filled the hall.

She burst into the gift-filled room
And squealed in glad surprise,
And all the Christmases-to-come
Were mirrored in her eyes.

How swiftly fly the rainbow years,
Like splintered shafts of light,
As fragile as the gentle ghosts
Who whisper in the night.

I draw my child into my arms
And hold this moment fast
Against the time my face will be
Her Ghost-of-Christmas Past.

ABOUT THE AUTHOR

Raised in Warrendale, Pennsylvania along with her brother, Amy Marshall lives where the past is still happening on five happy acres of family land. Her family grew strawberries there until 1974. She has a full-time career as a piano tuner, technician, and rebuilder, which she says finances her farming habit. Educated at the Sims School of Piano Technology and trained at Steinway and Sons, New York, Amy has been restoring and tuning pianos since 1977. During that time, she has raised two children, who have both carried the family tradition of growing food into their lives. Her son, Phil is a tomato breeder and seed farmer. Amy plays piano and works on her writing when she is not in the kitchen or the garden. Her husband Vince owns a business, and rebuilds pianos with her, works in the garden and does canning, harvests game on their land, and listens to her stories and book ideas. Christian faith motivates and gives purpose to all her pursuits. Responsible stewardship of the land and the soil are part of her faith practice, showing reverence for Creation and The Creator.

Recipes from Where the Past Is Still Happening

Amy Marshall

CONTENTS

Soups and Stews

Side Dishes

Main Dishes

INTRODUCTION

This is not a cookbook designed for convenience. It is designed to provide recipes for preparing timeless, real food. Gardening or marketing for fresh food is merely a type of cooking but with a grand vision. Growing food is a human activity, a pursuit that binds us to time and place.

Cooking is where all cultures come full circle generation to generation. For over sixty years, I have been preparing and sharing the recipes in this book. They are always best if made from fresh ingredients, but feel free to use frozen or canned if you must. The results are still spectacular!

I am unable to discern if my recipes are thrifty or extravagant, for survival or for feast, but they come from the earth, were formed in times of need, and are intended to delight. Enjoy!

Appetizers

Black Bean Dip

*Break out the corn tortilla chips and make a
margarita to go with this hot appetizer.*

Large iron skillet (or ovenproof casserole)
Makes 8 servings
Preheat oven to 350°F.

4 tablespoons bacon drippings or oil
32 ounces black beans, cooked or canned, liquid drained off
16 ounces salsa
2 garlic cloves, crushed
1 tablespoon ground cumin
1 cup shredded cheese, Monterey Jack, or Colby
1 cup sour cream
Zest of one lemon
Juice of one lemon
Fresh chives, chopped
Tortilla chips, if desired

Melt bacon drippings in the iron skillet. Place the beans in the skillet
and mash them with a potato masher to desired smoothness. Mix
in next four ingredients. Place in oven for 30 minutes or till heated
through and cheese is melted.

While bean dip is in the oven, mix the sour cream, lemon zest, and lemon juice together.

Remove bean dip from oven. Top with sour cream mixture and spread it out evenly. Top with fresh chives. Serve immediately.

Chicken Terrine

We made this for years and years. I never knew it was called a terrine until I had it in France. Traditionally served with breads, it is also wonderful with crudités. Chill a dry white wine and relax.

Makes 8 servings

1 quart chicken broth
1 whole chicken
2 bay leaves
2 tablespoons Herbes de Provence, tied in a small bag or in a tea ball
1 small onion chopped
1 cup real mayonnaise
2 tablespoons liquid from capers
1 teaspoon tarragon
1 ounce mayonnaise
1 teaspoon Grey Poupon Dijon Mustard
1/4 teaspoon cayenne pepper
Coarse black pepper
1/4 cup capers, drained

Wash chicken and discard liver and gizzards. Place the container of Herbes de Provence and the bay leaves inside the chicken cavity. Place the chicken in a Dutch oven or stew pot and pour the chicken broth over it. Bring just to a simmer, then reduce heat just a little. Poach the chicken gently without boiling for 2–3 hours till the meat falls off the bone.

Drain the chicken, discard the herbs and leaves, reserving the wonderful broth for another purpose such as consommé; it will even be strong enough to make an aspic.

When cool enough to handle, bone, skin, and cube the chicken meat. In a blender or food processor, grind the chicken meat and the onion till very fine. In a bowl, mix the meat, 1 cup mayonnaise, the caper liquid, and the tarragon. Chill for one hour.

Select a beautiful serving plate, preferably oval or rectangular. On it, form the chilled meat mixture into a loaf about 1 inch tall with a flat top. In a cup, whisk together the ounce of mayonnaise, the mustard, and the cayenne pepper. Spread this neatly on top of the flat loaf of chilled meat mixture. Sprinkle with black pepper.

Arrange the capers prettily on top, spilling onto the platter. Keep chilled until serving.

Cucumber Finger Sandwiches

When we have too many cucumbers, we make this fresh appetizer.
Maybe a Sunday afternoon tea is in order. Serve these with a cold
soup and fresh brewed tea. The ideal finish is Amy's Tea Cakes!

Makes 4 servings

4 ounces butter, softened
16 ounces cream cheese or Neufchatel cheese, softened
1 1/2 cups peeled and seeded cucumber, minced
1/4 cup chives, finely minced
1/4 teaspoon garlic powder
1/4 teaspoon salt
1/4 teaspoon pepper
10 slices firm white bread
10 slices firm brown bread

Blend together the first seven ingredients. Spread evenly onto ten slices of brown bread, going all the way to the edges. Top each with a slice of white bread. Chill 30 minutes.

With a thin knife, carefully cut off the crusts (or you may leave the crust on if you like.) Cut each sandwich into quarters, either squares or triangles, as you prefer.

Chill for one hour or more, wrapped tightly to prevent them from drying out.

There are many pretty ways to serve finger sandwiches; you may make a tower, or rows, or even set them up on edge in a pinwheel design. Have fun!

Eggplant Tepinade

Try this easy dish as a spread or a side dish.
Wonderful with crusty bread.

Preheat oven to 350°F.

4 large ripe eggplants, peeled and cut in large cubes
1 large onion, minced very fine
1 whole head of fresh garlic, peeled and finely chopped
1 teaspoon cayenne pepper
1 teaspoon sage
1 teaspoon thyme
1/2 tablespoon salt
1/2 teaspoon black pepper
1 cup olive oil

In large skillet, sauté the eggplant, onion, and garlic in half of the olive oil. It will probably be totally absorbed by the eggplant.

When vegetables are tender, place the mixture in a large oven-going bowl or casserole, covered, and place in hot oven. Reduce heat to 300°F and bake for 2 hours, stirring once at 1 hour, adding the remaining olive oil. When it is very soft and creamy, it is done!

Keep at room temperature till serving.

Roasted Rabbit and Cheese Board

*The perfect start to a game dinner. Serve with dark
beer or hearty wine, or even apple cider.*

Roasted Rabbit and Cheese Board

Makes 8 servings
Preheat oven to 350°F.

2 large rabbits
4 cloves garlic, crushed
1/4 cup bacon drippings
1 tablespoon smoked salt
2 bunches fresh sage
4-ounce wedge of distinctive cheese, such as Roquefort or chèvre
4-ounce wedge of milder cheese, such as smoked gouda or cheddar
A varied assortment of sweet and sour pickled vegetables, such as cucumber pickles, pickled beets, cornichons, pickled onions, peppers

The night before roasting the rabbits, crush the garlic and cook till fragrant in the bacon drippings. Add the smoked salt and massage the garlic mixture all over the rabbits. Place 1 bunch of sage in each cavity. Pour remaining drippings on the rabbits. Place them in a covered roasting pan in the refrigerator overnight.

The next day, put 1 cup of water in the bottom of the pan and place the pan of rabbits in the oven. Roast for 1 hour covered. Uncover them, baste with drippings, and roast uncovered for 30 more minutes. Remove to rack to cool. Chill before carving.

To Assemble the Board

Quarter the rabbits. Cut each of the 4 legs into two pieces. Remove the meat from the upper breast quarters in the biggest pieces possible, which will be dainty, and discard the bones. If any of the pieces are large enough to slice, slice them uniformly into attractive bite-size pieces. On a large rustic cutting or serving board, place the wedges of cheese; around them, display the cut-up roasted rabbit pieces and pretty little ramekins of assorted pickles. Sprinkle just a few grains of smoked salt onto the sliced rabbit portions.

Scotch Eggs

Very old-world

Scotch Eggs

A wooden or bamboo skewer
Makes 8 servings

8 hard-boiled eggs, just underdone
1 pound breakfast sausage meat, uncooked
2 raw eggs, slightly beaten
Flour
Bread crumbs
Oil for frying

Separate the sausage meat into 8 equal portions and flatten each into a thin patty large enough to wrap around 1 egg. Set aside. Prepare hard-boiled eggs, stopping the cooking time 3 minutes short, and plunging the eggs into cold water to stop the cooking. Peel the eggs when quite cold. Dip in flour. Wrap each egg in sausage, making sure each egg is totally encased in meat. Chill till meat is firm. Reshape if flat on one side.

Dip each meat-covered egg in beaten raw egg, then coat with bread crumbs. Press the crumbs into the sausage.

Heat the oil to 375°F in a small deep saucepan, deep enough to submerge a Scotch egg. Insert the wooden or bamboo skewer into the egg and lower it into the oil. Fry until dark golden brown. Use the skewer to draw the egg from the hot oil. Pull skewer out carefully. Place eggs on paper towels to drain. Cut in halves or serve whole, hot or cold. Serve with salt and pepper and hot sauce if you like.

Smoked Salmon on the Grill

This recipe is for cooked, smoked salmon, not cold-smoked salmon for preserving. Whether serving it warm or cold, presenting the fish whole or flaked as an appetizer or a meal, this versatile dish is always a hit.

A BBQ grill, with a lid
Wood for smoking (apple preferred)
Heavy-duty aluminum foil
Makes 3 pounds of smoked fish

Heat the BBQ grill to between 200-250ºF. If using charcoal, the coals should be a mature bed spread out to give low heat. At least 1 hour before smoking, place the applewood chips or chunks in a container of water to cover.

1 whole salmon, 4–5 pounds, head on, gutted and washed
10 limes
Olive oil
2 bunches fresh dill weed
1 cup minced onion
6 ounces capers, drained
8 hard-boiled eggs, peeled and chopped
1 cup real mayonnaise, in a small serving bowl

Part 1: Prepare and Smoke the Fish

Cut 8 of the limes in half, then slice the lime halves uniformly into neat half circles. Set aside. Juice the other 2 limes. Use the juice to bathe the inside of the fish cavity, then place the dill weed bunches inside the fish. Rub the entire fish on both sides with oil.

138

Place the fish on a large sheet of aluminum foil, large enough to fold over the top. Starting at the neck of the fish, layer the lime slices in overlapping rows to imitate scales, stopping at the tail to leave it exposed. Carefully, so as not to disturb the lime slices, fold the foil over and seal tightly. Wrap the entire fish package in a second layer of foil and seal tightly.

Place the wrapped fish, limes side down, on the grill on low heat and close lid. Cook for 15 minutes. Open the grill and place the wet apple wood in the coals or near the gas burners. Slice open the foil, exposing the side of the fish (without the lime slices). Carefully flip the fish onto the grill so that the lime side is up and gently remove the foil. Drizzle the fish with oil if desired. Close the lid and smoke the fish for 30 minutes. If the production of smoke slows down, remoisten the wood. Make sure the wood does not catch fire. If it does, wet the chips to extinguish the flames and produce smoke.

Remove the fish from the grill carefully to keep it from breaking apart. Place it on a board or attractive platter. Cover with new foil tightly and allow to rest for 30 minutes. At this time, the fish will be fully cooked.

Part 2: Serve the Fish, either Whole or Boned

At this point, you may choose to serve the whole fish. Make the dramatic presentation and in front of your guests, with a fork, peel back the lime "scales" and the top skin, exposing the succulent pink salmon. Either you or the guests may serve by flaking slabs of fish off the bones. When the top is "empty," flip the fish over and remove the skin and enjoy the second side.

Alternatively, you may choose to remove all the fish from the bones and flake onto a serving dish to serve.

Either way, alongside the served fish, present a platter on which is arranged the bowl of mayonnaise, and in 3 rows or heaps, the chopped eggs, the chopped onions, and the capers.

White Bean Dip

When the garden is full of green beans and bell peppers,
slice them up and dip them in this dense spread.

Makes 8 servings

3 tablespoons fresh lime juice (lemon will do)
2 tablespoons olive oil
1 teaspoon cumin
1/2 teaspoon tandoori spice or curry powder
2 garlic cloves, finely minced
4 cups cooked navy, white lima, or other tender white beans, drained
1 jalapeno pepper, seeded and minced
1/2 teaspoon salt
1/4 cup green onions, including tops, finely minced
3/4 cup red bell pepper, finely minced
3/4 cup minced fresh cilantro

Place everything, except the last 3 ingredients, in a food processor and pulse till smooth. Stir in the reserved peppers and onions, garnish with cilantro, and serve.

Salads and
Salad Dressings

Beet and Arugula Salad

A salad like this is the highlight of any meal. So satisfying, you can serve this salad as a main dish for your vegetarian friends. Just make the portions a little larger and serve with fresh bread.

Beet and Arugula Salad

Makes 4 servings

8 ounces mascarpone cheese, softened
1 lime, zested and juiced
2 ounces honey
4 medium-sized beets, cooked, peeled, and chilled, cut into wedges
2 cups fresh arugula
1/2 cup pistachio nuts, chopped
Balsamic vinegar
Olive oil
Coarse salt

Part 1: Prepare the Cheese

Soften the cheese and whip into it the honey, 2 tablespoons of lime juice, and 1 teaspoon of lime zest. Set aside at room temperature.

Part 2: Prepare the Beets

Wash the beets and cut off the tops and roots. Place in a pot and cover with water. Simmer on low until beets are fork-tender but not mushy. Immediately place them in cold water with some ice to stop them from continuing to cook. Peel them by gently rubbing off the peels. Rinse with cold water. Cut into uniform wedges, each beet making 6 nice wedges.

Part 3: Assemble the Salads

Have four large salad plates. On each plate, spread 2 ounces of the cheese mixture in a line across the middle of the plate, about 1-inch wide, leaving room for the greens on either side of the cheese. Place 1/2 cup of the arugula greens on each plate surrounding the cheese. Press the beet wedges, thin side down, into the cheese to form a fan. Sprinkle each beet fan and the greens with lime juice and salt. Top each salad with 1 ounce of pistachio nuts. Drizzle entire salad sparingly with balsamic vinegar and olive oil. Serve at room temperature or chilled.

Beet and Lemon Slaw

This is an unforgettable beet experience.
Turns the humble beet into royalty.

Makes 4 servings
4 raw medium-sized beets, peeled and shredded
Juice of two lemons
1 ounce avocado oil, grape seed oil, or canola oil
Salt and pepper

Mix all the ingredients together, place in refrigerator and allow to marry for about 1 hour.

Caprese Salad

Rush ripe, sun-warmed tomatoes from the garden to the salad platter. Grab a fistful of basil on the way.

Makes 4 servings

1 clove garlic, peeled and split in half
4 large ripe tomatoes, sliced
2 cups fresh basil leaves
1 pound buffalo (fresh) mozzarella cheese, sliced
Olive oil
Balsamic vinegar
Salt and pepper

Wash the tomatoes and basil in tepid—not cold—water. Dry the basil in a spinner or with paper towels. Take 1/2 of the garlic clove and rub the salad platter or plates sparingly with a few strokes. Discard the garlic.

On the prepared platter or on 4 prepared individual salad plates, arrange the tomatoes, basil, and cheese in alternating, overlapping layers. Make sure that the pretty basil leaves show. Drizzle with olive oil and balsamic vinegar. Salt and pepper to taste. Do not chill. Serve at room temperature.

Christmas Cranberry Salad

Is it a salad or a side dish? We have it every Thanksgiving and Christmas. So fresh, fruity, and crunchy, with a rich, creamy topping. It takes a little planning, as you have to prepare the fruit two weeks ahead.

Makes 8 servings

Part 1: Prepare Cranberry/Orange Relish

Two weeks before assembling the salad, make this relish. It is an ingredient in the salad.

1 pound fresh or frozen cranberries
2 oranges, not peeled, cut in chunks
2 cups white sugar

Wash the oranges and the cranberries. In a food processor, grind the cranberries and oranges, peels and all, coarsely. Mix in the sugar. Place in an airtight container and refrigerate for 2 weeks.

Part 2: Prepare the Salad

1 14 ounce can cranberry sauce (jellied type)
2 cups cranberry/orange relish
1/4 cup lemon juice
8 ounces red raspberry jam
2 cups apple, not peeled, chopped
2 cups celery, chopped
1 cup walnuts, chopped

In a saucepan, heat the canned cranberry sauce until melted. In a large bowl, combine the melted cranberry sauce and the next 6 ingredients. Place in a pretty serving bowl; crystal or glass work well.

Part 3: Prepare the Topping and Finish the Salad

1 cup sour cream
1/2 cup real mayonnaise

In a small bowl, mix the sour cream and the mayonnaise. You may serve it beside the salad in a separate dish or top the salad before serving.

Clear Sweet and Sour Cole Slaw

Serve warm or cold, beside or even in a sandwich!

Makes 8 servings

1 medium-sized head of cabbage, thinly sliced
1 small onion, thinly sliced
1/2 cup apple cider vinegar
1/4 cup corn oil
2 tablespoons white sugar
1/2 teaspoon salt
1/4 teaspoon black pepper
1/2 teaspoon celery seed

Place the cabbage and onions in a large bowl. In a small nonaluminum saucepan, combine the last 6 ingredients. Heat and stir just until the sugar is dissolved and it is very hot, but do not boil. While hot, pour the dressing over the cabbage and onions and mix well. Let stand at room temperature for 1 hour, stirring occasionally.

Serve warm or refrigerate.

Creamy Dilly Cole Slaw

Classic coleslaw without the sugar.

Makes 8 servings

1 medium-sized head of fresh cabbage, sliced thinly
1/2 small yellow onion, minced
1 clove garlic, crushed
1 ounce juice from dill pickles
1 teaspoon dill weed
1 teaspoon celery seed
3/4 cup real mayonnaise
Salt and pepper to taste

Place first two ingredients in a large bowl. In another bowl, mix together the last 6 ingredients to make a dressing. Pour the dressing on the cabbage and onions and stir well. Refrigerate for a minimum of 1 hour, stirring occasionally.

Serve in a pretty bowl, sprinkled with paprika or black pepper or top with sliced tomatoes and a sprig of parsley.

German Lettuce

A sweet and sour highlight, especially nice with
sauerkraut and pork or pierogies.

Makes 4 servings

1 head of iceberg lettuce, torn into bite-size pieces
4 strips of bacon, cooked till crispy, chopped into bits
1 large onion, cut in half then sliced thinly
3/4 cup red wine vinegar
1/4 cup melted bacon drippings
3 tablespoons sugar
Fresh ground black pepper

Place the torn iceberg lettuce in a large nonplastic bowl. Sprinkle the bacon bits over it.

In a large skillet, heat the bacon drippings and add the onions. Cook till translucent but still firm. Do not allow to brown. Add the vinegar and the sugar, simmer on low just till the sugar dissolves. While hot, pour over the lettuce and bacon mixture. Toss till the lettuce is well coated. Top with fresh ground black pepper and serve immediately while still warm.

Greek Salad

Dramatic, aromatic, and lovely to look at.
Add a few pitas and call it a meal!

A large flat platter
Makes 4 servings

1/4 cup olive oil
1/4 cup red wine vinegar
1 tablespoon dried oregano
1/2 teaspoon salt
1 clove fresh garlic, crushed
1 head romaine lettuce, cut into very thin ribbons
1 cup fresh basil, cut into very thin ribbons
1 green bell pepper, cored and seeded, sliced thinly into whole pepper rings
1 medium onion, sliced into thin slices, separated into rings
4 very ripe medium tomatoes, sliced very thin
1 cup feta cheese, crumbled
1 cup kalamata olives
4–8 pepperoncini peppers
Black pepper

Part 1: Make the Dressing

About 1 hour before assembling the salad, mix the first 5 ingredients in a medium bowl to make a dressing. Place the green pepper rings and onion rings into the bowl of dressing. Push them down gently to make sure they are submerged. Set aside and allow to marinate for 1 hour.

Part 2: Assemble the Salad

Spread out the romaine and the basil on the platter to make a thin even bed. Around the edge, lay out the thin tomato slices in a circle. Also place a few slices in the center of the bed of greens.

Take the marinated onion and pepper rings out of the dressing (do not discard the dressing) and lay them in an even layer on top of the tomatoes and greens, letting the tomatoes show around the edges. On top of the onion and pepper layer, sprinkle the feta cheese evenly. Distribute the olives on top of the cheese, placing most of them in the center. Place the pepperoncini on top to garnish. Pour the reserved dressing over all. Top with a dusting of black pepper. Serve at room temperature.

Mexican Bean Salad

On a hot summer evening, try this salad as a main dish.
It's hearty enough to be a meal in itself. After you put
this salad together, you will have time for a siesta!

Makes 4 servings as a main dish
Makes 8 servings as a salad

Part 1: Prepare Salad

2 large fresh tomatoes, chopped
1 sweet bell pepper, seeded and chopped
1 jalapeno pepper, seeded and minced
1 medium onion, chopped
2 cups kidney beans or black beans (cooked, or canned, not dry), drained
1 cup corn, fresh or frozen, cooked and chilled
1 cup shredded or cubed Monterey Jack cheese
1 tablespoon whole cumin seeds
1 teaspoon chili powder
2 tablespoons lime juice

Combine all 10 salad ingredients in a large bowl. Toss to mix.

Part 2: Prepare Dressing and Complete Salad

1 cup sour cream or Greek yogurt or a mixture of both
1 cup salsa
Fresh cilantro

In another bowl, mix the dairy product of your choice with the salsa. Top with fresh cilantro. Mix the dressing into the salad or serve separately.

Peachy Garden Salad

When the peaches and cucumbers get ripe, you should still have radishes and collards or other greens on hand in the garden.

Makes 4 servings

Part 1: Prepare the Dressing

1 tablespoon honey
1/2 teaspoon dried or 1 teaspoon fresh grated ginger
2 tablespoon soy sauce
1/4 cup balsamic vinegar
2 tablespoon oil
1/4 teaspoon minced garlic
1/2 teaspoon salt

Mix all dressing ingredients together and let marry while preparing the vegetables and fruit.

Part 2: Complete the Salad

4 cups fresh baby collards or other greens, cut fine, or torn lettuce
2 ripe peaches, cubed
1 large cucumber, cubed
12 large radishes, sliced
1 teaspoon black sesame seed

Toss all together with the dressing just before serving.

Sauerkraut Garden Salad

Easy, fresh, and surprising.

Makes 4 servings

4 cups lettuce, spinach, chard, or any other fresh greens, torn
4 large tomatoes, chopped
1 cucumber, chopped
1 medium onion, diced
1–2 cups any other fresh garden vegetables you wish to add, such as radishes, green beans, snow peas, etc.
1–2 cups drained, uncooked sauerkraut (do not used canned; if you don't make your own, try to buy live, fresh sauerkraut)

Combine all ingredients in a large bowl. Toss lightly. Chill for about 30 minutes. Toss again and serve. Needs no dressing as the sauerkraut is the dressing!

True French Dressing

*This bold but simple dressing is served in France. Salad
is usually a last course served with wine and bread.*

4 tablespoons Grey Poupon Dijon Mustard
2 ounces olive oil
2 ounces flavorful vinegar (such as apple cider, champagne wine, red
wine)
2 tablespoons water
1 teaspoon salt
1/2 teaspoon pepper

Place all ingredients in a jar or carafe and mix well.

Black Raspberry Vinaigrette

*Dress any salad with this vinaigrette, but it is especially
well suited to any salad made with fruit or nuts.*

3 ounces balsamic vinegar
2 ounces olive oil
2 tablespoons water
3 tablespoons black raspberry syrup
1/2 teaspoon salt
1/4 teaspoon black pepper
1/4 teaspoon garlic powder
1/4 teaspoon ground thyme

Combine all the ingredients in a jar or carafe. Mix well. Allow to
marry for at least 30 minutes before serving.

Lemon Vinaigrette

Peppy and fragrant, a refreshing dressing winter or summer.

2 lemons, juiced, seeds strained out
1 tablespoon lemon zest
1 ounce grape seed, avocado, safflower, or other light-flavored oil
1 tablespoon water
1 teaspoon salt
1/2 teaspoon white sugar
1/2 teaspoon tarragon
1/2 teaspoon pepper

Combine all the ingredients in a jar or carafe. Mix well. Allow to marry for at least 30 minutes before serving.

Soups and Stews

Asparagus Soup

A creamy, chunky bright green soup. Adding the raw spinach
and asparagus tips at the very end is the secret to a soup
that tastes garden fresh and has a bright green color.

Makes 1 to 2 quarts

3 cups vegetable stock, homemade if possible
1 pound of fresh asparagus, woody stem ends snapped off and cut in
1-inch pieces
1 cup fresh asparagus tips chopped
2 tablespoons fresh squeezed lemon juice
2 small onions, diced
2 cloves garlic, chopped
4 small red potatoes, skins on, cut up
2 cups fresh spinach
4 tablespoons butter
1/4 cup sour cream
Salt and pepper to taste

Break off stem ends of asparagus. In a medium pot, combine the
stock and the stem ends of the asparagus and simmer for 30 minutes.
Remove stems with a slotted spoon and discard. Add lemon juice.

In a large pot, brown onions and garlic in butter. Add the asparagus
pieces and the potatoes. Reserve the raw spinach and the asparagus
tips. Add the vegetable stock and bring to simmer.

Simmer gently 30 minutes.

Place hot mixture and raw spinach in food processor and pulse till
smooth. Return to pot, add sour cream and salt and pepper. Stir in
asparagus tips and reheat soup but do not overcook.

Corn Chowder

Rich and comforting, we freeze this soup for a quick meal on a cold winter night. Feel free to make a smaller batch to eat right away!

Makes 10 quarts

3 1/2 dozen ears of sweet corn
10 cups water (approximately)
3/4 pound butter
1 large onion, minced
4 cups whole milk
1/4 cup corn starch
1 dozen hard-boiled eggs, peeled and chopped fine
1 tablespoon salt
1 tablespoon white pepper
1 teaspoon dried mustard

Cut corn kernels from the cobs and set aside in a bowl. Break in half and place cobs in a large stock pot and add just enough water to cover, about ten cups. Bring to a boil, reduce to a simmer for an hour or two to make a corn stock (a corny joke!).

In a smaller pot, sauté the onions in the butter till soft but not browned. Add the corn starch to the butter and onions, add 1 cup of milk. Stir till thick; add the rest of the milk 1 cup at a time.

Remove the cobs from the stock and discard the cobs. To the stock, add all the corn kernels and the milk mixture. Add the last 4 ingredients. Simmer on low for about 30 minutes.

Serve right away and freeze the rest in batches. Do not can.

Creamy, Dreamy Vegetable Soup

The name was given to this soup by my children. It was delightful when they would say, "Make your creamy dreamy vegetable soup, Mom!"

Makes 3 to 4 quarts

6 cups good vegetable stock
1 large onion
1 parsnip
1 large turnip
3 carrots
1 cup peas, fresh or frozen
4 cups spinach, chard, or kale
1 large potato, peeled
2 roasted sweet peppers
2 cups green beans
1 cup cabbage
1 bunch of parsley, chopped, no stems, leaves only
3 cloves garlic
2 bay leaves
1 cup fresh cream or sour cream
2 tablespoons butter or oil of choice
Salt and pepper to taste

Chop and place all vegetables in a large stock pot. Cover with stock. Bring to very gentle simmer (do not boil, which will lessen the delicate flavors of the vegetables.) After 1 hour, remove the bay leaves. Simmer for another hour, adding a little water if needed. The vegetables should just be covered in liquid.

Pulse in food processor or blender in batches till pureed. Return to pot; add butter, cream, salt and pepper.

Extraordinary Mushroom Soup

*People have called this soup sophisticated and
even extraordinary; I call it delicious.*

Makes 2 quarts

2 cups dried shitake mushrooms
2 cups fresh button mushrooms sliced thinly
2 cups fresh portabella mushrooms sliced thinly
1/4 cup sherry
1/4 cup port wine
1 large yellow onion, diced
1 small tomato diced
Juice of 1/2 lemon
3 bay leaves
4 cups chicken or vegetable broth
3 tablespoons Herbes de Provence
3 tablespoons olive oil
1 large white potato, boiled, peeled and cubed
1 teaspoon Worcestershire sauce
1/2 cup butter
Unbleached white flour
Salt and pepper
Sour cream and chopped fresh tomato (to garnish)

In a bowl, place dried shitake mushrooms in hot water, just to cover, and 1/4 cup sherry. Let soak for at least 1 hour. Place olive oil in the bottom of large soup pot; add diced onion, diced tomato, bay leaves, and herbes de Provence; and cook until onion begins to brown.

Add the broth and fresh mushrooms and let simmer about 1 hour until married. Add the cubed potato and the shitakes along with the soaking mixture, juice of 1/2 lemon, and salt and pepper to taste, Worcestershire sauce and let simmer 30 minutes more. Remove bay leaves, and add the port wine.

Prepare a butter and flour roux as follows: Melt the butter in a medium skillet and heat it till it is just turning golden brown. Add the flour a few tablespoons at a time, stirring constantly until a soft paste forms. Immediately remove from heat.

With the soup at a slow simmer, add half the roux, stirring the soup until it thickens. If you want it even thicker, repeat with the rest of the roux to reach desired thickness.

Just before serving, taste and adjust for salt and add more sherry or wine if desired. Serve topped with a dollop of sour cream and chopped fresh tomato.

Dumplings for Soup, Stew, or Sauerkraut

These fluffy dumplings are Grandma Ruth's recipe for making any soup meal hearty and fun. Don't be tempted to peek at the dumplings while they steam, or they will get soggy. Choose the fat you use for flavor or convenience.

Makes 4 servings

1 cup unbleached flour
1/2 teaspoon salt
1 1/2 teaspoon baking powder
1/2 cup milk
2 tablespoons fat (melted lard, bacon drippings, butter or oil of choice)

Optional additions to dumplings: After making the dough, you may add shredded cheese or bacon bits, minced onions, spices, or herbs. Mix the addition in quickly, without overworking the dough, just before steaming.

Sift together the dry ingredients. Make a well in the middle and add the milk and the fat. If it is a melted fat, let it cool a little before adding. Mix just long enough to make a soft, wet dough.

When your soup, stew, or sauerkraut dish is ready to serve, set it on low to just simmer. If it is boiling, it will ruin the dumplings. Drop the dumpling dough by medium-sized spoonsful onto the top of the liquid. They will float!

Cover tightly and allow to steam for about 15 minutes without lifting lid. Remove to a platter with a slotted spoon.

Herbed Mushroom Soup

Have herbs by the bunch? Use them to make the herbal broth that is the base for this decadent soup.

Makes 1 to 2 quarts

Part 1: Prepare Herbal Broth

5 cups water
1 large onion, quartered
1 sweet bell pepper, quartered
Celery stalks and leaves
Mushroom stems and scraps
6 bay leaves
1 or 2 large fistfuls of each, chives, thyme, sage, rosemary, parsley, tarragon, marjoram
1 sprig lavender
10 peppercorns
5 juniper berries
1 tablespoon salt

Combine the broth ingredients in a large soup pot and simmer on low for 2 hours. Strain out solids and discard.

Part 2: Prepare Herbed Mushroom Soup

4 ounces butter
4 cups sliced mushrooms, any variety
White or wheat flour

1 cup whole milk or cream
1/2 cup sour cream
1/4 cup port wine (or more!)
4 cups herbal broth

Melt the butter in a 4-quart soup pot. Add the sliced mushrooms and sauté till soft and fragrant. Remove mushrooms with slotted spoon and reserve in a bowl. Slowly sprinkle flour into the butter in the pan and stir over low heat until a thick paste is formed. Add milk or cream and stir until a very thick slurry is made. Add more milk if it gets too thick. To this thick mixture, add sour cream, herbal broth, mushrooms and port, in that order. Simmer gently but do not boil! Add salt to taste. Serve before port cooks off. If you have to hold the soup, you may add more port to taste just before serving. Garnish with finely chopped fresh herbs of your choice.

Phil's Best Black-Eyed Pea Soup Ever

Philip was just a young boy when he chose a vegetarian diet. In a family of meat lovers, he had to develop his own recipes. His sister named this one. Even an omnivore will love this soup.

Makes 3 to 4 quarts

1 pound of dried black-eyed peas
3 cups of tomato juice
2 large onions, minced
4 bay leaves
3 stalks celery, chopped finely
6 cloves garlic
1 teaspoon celery seed
1 teaspoon crushed hot red pepper, or 1/2 teaspoon cayenne pepper
Salt and pepper

Rinse black-eyed peas and soak 3 hours or overnight. Drain then add fresh water just to cover. Add all the other ingredients and simmer for 2 hours. Black-eyed peas should be very tender.

Ratatouille, Vegetarian

Garden fresh soup can be served chilled or hot.
Wonderful with a spoonful of jasmine rice.

Makes 1 quart

4 tablespoons olive oil
1 medium onion, thinly sliced
6 garlic cloves, minced
1 bay leaf
1 medium eggplant, peeled and cubed
1 small zucchini, halved and thinly sliced
1 red bell pepper, cut into slivers
4 whole medium tomatoes, coarsely chopped
1 teaspoon salt
1 cup shredded fresh basil leaves, no stems
1/4 cup fresh oregano, no stems
Fresh parsley
Black pepper

In a large pan, brown the onion and garlic in the oil. Add the eggplant and cook until softened. Stir in the zucchini, bell pepper, tomatoes, and salt. Cook over medium heat, stirring frequently for 5 to 7 minutes. Stir in the fresh basil and parsley. Add pepper to taste.

Spiced Tomato Soup

This wonderful, easy soup can be served hot or cold. Make it in the summer when tomatoes abound, or serve it all year long when you crave that Mediterranean flare.

Makes 1 quart

1 small onion
1 clove garlic
3 tablespoons olive oil
2 tablespoons paprika
1/2 teaspoon ground ginger
1/2 teaspoon ground cumin
1/2 teaspoon tarragon
1/2 teaspoon ground cinnamon
1 teaspoon curry powder
1 1/2 cups chicken or vegetable broth
32 ounces fresh tomatoes, chopped small
2 teaspoons honey
2 tablespoons fresh parsley, chopped
2 tablespoons fresh cilantro, chopped
1 teaspoon lime juice
Salt and pepper to taste

Cook onion in oil with spices in a 3- or 4-quart heavy pan over moderate heat, stirring occasionally until onion is softened and begins to brown, about 4–5 minutes. Add the chopped tomatoes (with their juices), honey, 1/2 of the parsley, 1/2 of the cilantro. Bring to a boil. Immediately transfer to a large metal bowl or pan set in a larger bowl or sink full of ice. Cool soup, stirring occasionally for about 15–20 minutes. Stir in lime juice, the remainder of the parsley and cilantro. Add salt and pepper to taste.

Vegetable Stock

*Making good stock and keeping it on hand is a good
practice and makes use of leftovers. Do you have too many
fresh veggies from the garden today? Make stock!*

Makes about 3 quarts

1 large onion, cut up in pieces
8 cups raw, or raw and cooked vegetables, such as, but not limited
to, celery, onions, onion tops, leeks, green beans, carrots, turnips,
parsnips, peppers, mushrooms, zucchini, etc.
6 peppercorns
4 tablespoons high quality oil
12 cups cold water
Salt to taste

Heat oil and brown the onion. Add the other vegetables and water to
cover. Place over low heat and bring slowly to a simmer. Don't rush
or it may make a bitter stock.

Simmer for 2 hours or more, adding water if needed to maintain
volume.

Strain through colander or colander lined with cheesecloth for a clear
stock.

Refrigerate for up to 2 days or freeze.

Venison Stew

*This stew works great in a crock pot. If you choose
to cook it on the stove, cook it long and slow so the
meat will be melt-in-your-mouth tender.*

Makes 2 quarts

1 pound cubed venison (you can substitute beef or lamb)
3 medium potatoes, peeled and cubed
1 large onion, diced
4 carrots, sliced
4 garlic cloves, minced
2 cloves
1 bay leaf
2 cups red wine
Salt and pepper
1/4 cup flour
1 cup water

Place all but the last 2 ingredients in the slow cooker or crock pot. Turn to low and leave for 8 hours. Remove lid, stir gently.

Mix the flour and water together with a whisk till there are no lumps. Stir into the stew. Cover and cook for 10 minutes to thicken. Adjust for salt and pepper to taste. Remove cloves and bay leaf before serving.

Winter Squash Stew

*Whether you grow your own squash or buy it, this is
a healthy and economical main dish. A nice savory
change from traditionally sweet squash soups.*

Makes 2 to 3 quarts
Preheat oven to 350°F.

2 or 3 winter squash, can be mixed varieties such as acorn, butternut,
hubbard, or even pumpkin (about 4 cups when cubed)
2 cups peeled and cubed potatoes
4 cups chicken, turkey or vegetable stock
1 bay leaf
1 cup mushrooms, sliced
1 large onion, minced
1/4 cup butter
2 tablespoons turmeric
1 tablespoon coriander
1/2 teaspoon cardamom
Salt and pepper

Prick squash and place in 350°F degree oven. Roast just until easy to
cut up. Cool, peel, remove seeds, and cut into bite-size cubes. It is
really nice if the cubes of squash and potatoes are the same size.

In a medium-sized pot, heat the bay leaf and the sliced mushrooms
in the stock until mushrooms are tender.

In a large heavy pot, brown the onions in the olive oil till golden and caramelized. Add the turmeric, coriander, cardamom, salt, and pepper. Add the cubes of squash and potatoes. Add the broth and mushroom mixture.

Simmer until the squash and potatoes are tender but not mushy. Remove the bay leaf and serve.

Note: If you have more cubed squash than you need, freeze it. It makes a great side dish just cooked till tender and served with salt and pepper or a little cinnamon.

Yellow Tomato and Squash Soup

A rich but light summery soup, golden in color.

Makes 2 quarts

1/2 cup butter
4 cups yellow tomatoes, peeled and chopped
1 yellow bell pepper, chopped fine
1 large onion, chopped fine
2 tablespoons lemon juice
1 teaspoon marjoram
4 cups cooked mashed acorn, butternut or other squash, even pumpkin
1 teaspoon salt
1/2 teaspoon white pepper
2 cups cooked white rice

Melt the butter in a large soup pot. Add the onion, yellow pepper, lemon juice, and marjoram and sauté till soft and fragrant. Add the tomatoes and mashed squash and heat to a simmer. Add salt and pepper. Stir in the rice just before serving.

Side Dishes

Aunt Orie's Dandelion Pie

*Even after my Aunt Orie came to live with us at The House,
she still made dandelion pie each spring, just like our family
had for generations. Ensure that no chemicals have been applied
to the area where the dandelions have been harvested.*

A deep baking dish, preferably round
Makes 4 servings
Preheat oven to 350°F.

12 large young dandelion leaves, left whole
4 cups tender young dandelion leaves, washed and chopped
1 pound ricotta cheese
4 eggs
4 slices toasted, buttered bread, chopped into cubes
1 small onion, minced
4 cloves garlic, minced

Butter the baking dish well, making sure to cover the sides and the bottom. Arrange the 12 dandelion leaves in a clock or pinwheel design, overlapping neatly. Set aside.

In a large bowl, combine all the other ingredients. Spoon them gently over the arranged dandelion leaves so as not to disturb. Cover with a plate and bake for 45 minutes. Remove from oven and allow to rest for 20 minutes. When plate is cool enough to touch, carefully invert the plate and casserole to unmold pie onto plate.

If you don't have time or don't feel fancy, just chop all the dandelions and mix all ingredients and bake as directed. Serve from baking dish.

Bernie's Swiss Corn Bake

My father loved Swiss cheese. This is a chewy
cheese and corn lover's dream come true.

Makes 4 servings

4 cups corn kernels, fresh or frozen
1/2 cup onion, minced
1 1/2 cups Swiss cheese, shredded
10 ounces heavy cream
1 tablespoon brown mustard
1/4 teaspoon salt
1/2 cup bread crumbs
4 tablespoons melted butter

If using frozen corn, thaw it by rinsing with hot water. Drain well.
Place the corn and all the ingredients in a casserole dish and mix well.
Top with bread crumbs. Drizzle with butter. Place in oven for 30
minutes till cheese is melted and top is beginning to brown. Remove
from oven and allow to rest for 5 minutes.

Fresh Green Bean Casserole

This recipe goes back to a time before canned soup and canned beans; it makes you love green beans again.

Fresh Green Bean Casserole, Great Grandma's Tablecloth

Large casserole dish
Makes 8 servings
Preheat oven to 350°F.

4 cups fresh green beans, trimmed and cut into 1- to 2-inch pieces
1 cup fresh mushrooms, sliced
1 1/2 cups cream

2 tablespoons white flour
1/2 teaspoon salt
2 tablespoons oil
1 clove garlic, minced
4 tablespoons butter
1 large onion, sliced into thin ribbons

In a large pot, bring 4 cups of water to a boil. Blanch the green beans in the boiling water for 2 minutes. Drain well and place the beans into the casserole dish, add the mushrooms. Set aside.

In a small bowl, whisk the flour, salt, oil, and garlic into the cream. Pour over the beans. Place in 350°F oven for 45 minutes and bake till bubbly.

While beans are baking, heat the butter in a skillet. Fry the onions till crispy, brown and fragrant.

Top the bubbling green bean casserole piled high with the crispy fried onions. Serve immediately.

Mashed Rutabagas

Sweeter than mashed potatoes and just as comforting.

Makes 8 servings

2 large rutabagas, peeled and cubed
1/2 cup sour cream
Salt and pepper

Place the cubed rutabagas in a heavy pot and cover with water. Bring to a boil and partially cover the pot. Boil gently for about 1 hour until fork-tender.

Drain well and return to the warm pot. Mash with a potato masher and mix in the sour cream and salt to taste. They will be light and fluffy.

Top with a little butter and black pepper when serving if desired.

Parsley Potatoes

*If you love pure potato flavor, then you will love these.
Your mouth will water as you run with them from the
field to the kitchen. Grab your parsley on the way!*

Makes 4 servings

2 pounds small red-skinned or other new potatoes, skins on, halved
1 cup fresh parsley, stems removed and chopped fine
1/4 cup butter (or more)
Salt and pepper

Wash the potatoes thoroughly. Cut in half. Do not peel. Drop them
into a pot of boiling water and simmer gently for about 30 minutes or till tender all the way through but firm and not falling apart.
Drain the potatoes and return to hot pot. Add the butter, parsley, and
salt and pepper to taste. Toss gently till butter is melted and coats the
potatoes. Serve immediately.

Pasta Prima Vera

*In Italian, primavera means "spring." I think of the first green things
I can pull from the garden, but I keep making this all summer long!*

Makes 8 servings as a side dish, 4 servings as a main dish

1 pound fettuccini noodles
4 cups fresh raw green vegetables, such as chard, dandelion, scallions,
garlic scapes, spinach, peas, snow peas, asparagus, green beans, zucchini washed and cut into bite-size pieces
1/2 cup fresh basil leaves
2 cloves fresh garlic, crushed
1/2 cup olive oil
1 cup shredded asiago cheese
2 ounces grated parmesan cheese
2 ounces Romano cheese
Parsley, basil, capers, or green olives to garnish

Prepare the pasta, boiling it until desired tenderness. I prefer al dente.

Before draining the pasta, drop all the raw vegetables into the boiling
water and stir into the pasta for 1 minute till bright green.

Drain pasta and vegetables and place in a large pasta dish or flat serving bowl. Add the garlic, basil, olive oil, and cheeses and stir gently so
the vegetables are evenly distributed. If it seems dry, add some more
olive oil. Garnish. Serve at room temperature.

Scalloped Potatoes

An Easter must-have, perfect with ham.

A large casserole or roasting pan
Makes 8 servings
Preheat oven 350°F.

4 pounds potatoes, peeled and sliced very thin
1 large onion, halved and sliced into very thin half rings
1 green bell pepper, halved and sliced into very thin half rings
1 cup mushrooms sliced or chopped
1/2 cup butter
2 cups heavy cream, cold
1/4 cup white flour
1/2 teaspoon salt
1/4 teaspoon pepper
Paprika
Optional: 1/2 cup shredded white cheddar cheese

In a bowl, mix together the onions, green pepper and mushrooms. In the casserole or roasting pan, make a layer of potato slices using about 1/3 of the potatoes. On top of that, make a layer of onions, peppers, and mushrooms, using about 1/3. Repeat layering potatoes and vegetables till pan is full, ending with the onions, peppers, and mushrooms on the top.

In a medium bowl, whisk the flour into the cold cream till there are no lumps. Add the salt and pepper. In a large saucepan, melt the butter. Pour in the cream mixture, stirring constantly with a wooden spoon over low heat till it begins to thicken. Pour into the casserole over the potatoes and vegetables. Top with cheese if using. Sprinkle with paprika. Cover tightly and place in 350°F oven for 90 minutes till potatoes are fork tender.

Main Dishes

All-Day Venison Roast with Root Vegetables

Bring out a few shoulders, necks, or whatever venison roasts you have. If you do just one, it won't be the same succulent experience. This will feed a large group, or you can bone the roasts after they cool and make sandwiches; we freeze the tender fall-off-the-bone meat in one-pound packages for future use in tacos, burritos, chili, or whatever you desire.

2 large roasting pans with lids, greased
Serves 4 per roast

4 venison shoulder or neck roasts (about 3 to 4 pounds each)
1/2 cup horseradish
1/2 cup Grey Poupon Dijon Mustard
1/2 cup olive oil
1 teaspoon salt
1 teaspoon pepper
8 cloves garlic crushed
2 tablespoons rosemary
2 teaspoons thyme

Per roasting pan:

2 onions, peeled and quartered
2 potatoes, peeled and quartered
2 turnips, peeled and halved
2 parsnips, peeled and halved

4 carrots, peeled and quartered
2 beets, peeled and quartered
2 cups red wine
2 cloves

Arrange your roasts in the greased roasting pans. In a medium bowl, mix the next 8 ingredients together. Massage this mixture over the roasts on all sides till well covered. Pour any remaining over the top of it all. Nestle all the vegetables around and atop the roasts evenly. Pour the red wine gently between the roasts in both pans, trying not to wash the horseradish mixture off the meat. Drop the cloves down into the liquid.

Cover tightly. Place in 375°F oven for 30 minutes. Reduce heat to 325°F and roast for 3 hours. Reduce to 300°F and roast for 1 more hour.

Check the roasts at this point; meat should be falling off the bone. If not, make sure there is still a lot of liquid in the bottom, adding a little water or more wine if needed, cover tightly again and roast at 300°F for 30 minutes to 1 hour.

Remove meat to large platter and place the vegetables in large bowls with the liquid.

Make a dramatic "hunter's" presentation, letting the guests pull the meat from the bones. Be sure to have lots of crusty bread to sop up the juices!

Braised Venison Shanks

Your kitchen will be filled with the tantalizing aroma
for hours while you slow braise these tender shanks.

A large roasting pan with a lid
Each shank serves 1 person
Preheat oven to 350°F.

4–8 venison shanks
1/2 cup flour
1 tablespoon tarragon
4–8 tablespoons bacon drippings
1 quart vegetable or chicken stock
1 cup white wine
1 tablespoon vinegar or lemon juice
12 small onions, peeled and left whole
1 clove
6 peppercorns
4 garlic cloves
2 bay leaves
1 teaspoon tarragon
Olive oil
Salt and pepper

Bring the shanks out of the refrigerator and let stand to reach room
temperature. Mix the flour and the tarragon in a flat dish. Melt the
bacon drippings in a skillet. Dredge the shanks in the seasoned flour
and brown them, 1 or 2 at a time, in the bacon drippings. Remove
them from the skillet to the roasting pan. Cover the shanks with

the liquids, nestling the small onions around them. Place the clove, peppercorns, garlic, and bay leaves in the liquid. Sprinkle all with 1 teaspoon tarragon. Drizzle all with oil and dust with salt and pepper.

Place in the oven for 2 hours. Check periodically to make sure the liquids have not gone dry. Add more wine or broth if needed. Cover and bake for 1 to 2 more hours until the meat falls off the bone.

Place on a platter with the little onions. Serve with mashed potatoes. You can strain the liquid and serve as consommé or thicken it to use as gravy.

Mushroom and Herb Patties in Mornay Sauce

A company meal for sure. Great with a crisp white wine.

Makes 4 servings

Part 1: Prepare the Mornay Sauce

2 tablespoons butter
1 1/2 tablespoons flour
1 cup milk
1 cup heavy cream
1 bay leaf
2 tablespoons salt
1/4 teaspoon each of the following:
Pepper, thyme, sage, marjoram, rosemary, parsley, cayenne pepper
2 tablespoons sherry
Dash Worcestershire sauce
1/2 cup grated mild cheddar cheese

Melt the butter in saucepan over medium heat. Add flour and cook, stirring constantly til blended. Reduce heat to low. Add milk, cream, and bay leaf, whisking until sauce thickens, about 8 minutes. Stir in the remaining ingredients until smooth. Cover and keep warm. Remove bay leaf just before serving.

Part 2: Prepare the Cutlets

2 eggs
1 tablespoon salt
1/4 teaspoon each of the following:
Pepper, thyme, sage, marjoram, rosemary, parsley, cayenne pepper
1/2 teaspoon Worcestershire sauce
2 cups fresh mushrooms, chopped coarsely
2 scallions, trimmed and chopped fine
1 cup fresh bread crumbs
1 1/2 cups grated mild cheddar cheese
4 tablespoons butter

Beat together eggs, salt, pepper, herbs, and Worcestershire sauce in a large bowl. Mix in the mushrooms, scallions, bread crumbs, and cheese. Shape into 8 patties. Heat half the butter in a skillet over medium heat. Fry patties in 2 batches in the butter until crisp and brown, about 3 minutes per side.

Serve cutlets with sauce.

Orange-Cocoa Pork Loin

Really different, sparkly bright flavors; the cocoa lends depth.

Makes 6–8 servings
Preheat oven to 350°F.

1 whole pork loin, about 3 pounds
2 oranges, juiced
1/4 cup dark unsweetened cocoa powder
1 tablespoon rosemary leaves
1/2 teaspoon black pepper
1/4 cup Grey Poupon Dijon Mustard
1/4 cup olive oil
2 tablespoons fresh orange zest
1 tablespoon minced garlic

Place the pork loin in a shallow dish and pour the orange juice over it. Allow to marinate for about 30 minutes. Meanwhile, grease a roasting pan. Blend the cocoa powder and rosemary leaves together in a cup and set aside.

In a small bowl, mix the last 5 ingredients together.

Place the pork loin in the greased pan, and add the orange juice to the mustard mixture. Mix well. Coat the pork with 1/2 of the mustard/orange mixture and place in oven for 30 minutes. After 30 minutes, reduce heat to 325°F. Apply the remainder of the mixture to the meat. Dust thickly with the powdered cocoa and rosemary leaves.

Roast for 30 more minutes or till it reaches 140 internal temperature. If it cooks to above that temperature, it will be dry and tough. It is all right if the meat has a pinkish color as long as it reaches at least 140°F in the thickest part of the loin.

Remove from oven, sprinkle with fresh orange zest, and cover with foil. Allow to rest for 5 minutes.

Ruth's Curried Chicken, Cashews, and Currants

My daughter Ruth introduced this dish to me as a salad. I like it as a main dish. Try it and decide for yourself!

Makes 8 servings

1 whole chicken, boiled, skin removed, boned, and meat cubed
1 cup chopped celery
1 cup cashews
1 cup dried currants
3/4 cup real mayonnaise
3/4 cup Greek yogurt
2 tablespoons Madras curry powder (or more to taste)
1 teaspoon salt
1/2 teaspoon pepper
Juice of 1 lime
Fresh cilantro for garnish
Fresh lime wedges for garnish
Lettuce or fresh greens

In a large bowl combine all ingredients, except the last 3. Allow to marry for at least 30 minutes.

Serve warm or chilled on a bed of lettuce or greens, topped with cilantro and lime wedges.

Spicy BBQ Pulled Venison

Served on a bun or a bed of rice, this quick easy
meal is special. Serve with creamy coleslaw.

Makes 4 servings

1 pound venison cut-up in pieces (or substitute beef)
1 quart barbecue sauce
1 pint pickled hot peppers (your favorite kind)

Place all three ingredients in a slow cooker or Crock-Pot for 6 to 8 hours or simmer very low in a large heavy pot for 3 to 4 hours till meat shreds.

Shred meat and serve with sauce over rice or on buns.

Stuffed Pumpkin

Modify the fillings to suit your family; the process is fun and simple!

Makes 4 servings
Preheat oven to 350°F.

1 small pumpkin, about 10" in diameter
1 cup cooked rice
1 pound ground turkey (or ground beef, chicken, venison, pork)
2 tablespoons oil
2 eggs
1 small onion minced
2 cloves garlic, minced
1/2 cup peas or corn
1/2 teaspoon turmeric
1/2 teaspoon sage
1/2 teaspoon thyme
Salt and pepper to taste
A pat of butter

To prepare the pumpkin, wash it and cut a "lid" by cutting a circle around the stem about 3 inches from the stem. Remove the "lid" carefully. Scoop out the seeds and strings from the inside of the pumpkin with a spoon and either reserve them for another use or discard.

In a large bowl, combine all the filling ingredients together, mixing well with your hands. Place the filling inside the pumpkin by forming balls of filling and packing them in tightly. Place the "lid" back on the pumpkin. Prick the pumpkin in a few places to allow steam to escape and rub the outside of the whole pumpkin with butter.

Place the pumpkin in a baking dish. Bake in 350°F oven for 1 hour; reduce heat to 300°F and bake 30 more minutes until the pumpkin is toasty brown and fully cooked so a knife inserted goes through the pumpkin flesh easily.

Move the pumpkin to a serving platter, remove the "lid," and cut the pumpkin into 4 equal wedges to serve.

Zucchini Lasagna

The fun of this recipe is not needing to cook either the noodles or the zucchini before assembling. I use my homemade spaghetti sauce, tomato juice, and ricotta cheese when I have time. Otherwise, good organic ricotta cheese from the store works very well.

10-inch × 15-inch glass baking dish
Makes 8 servings
Preheat oven to 350°F.

2 eggs
2 cups ricotta cheese (see Homemade Ricotta Cheese below)
1 teaspoon dried basil
1 teaspoon dried oregano
1/2 teaspoon black pepper
1 pound box lasagna noodles, uncooked
1 large zucchini, ends trimmed, cut in thin "planks"
8 slices provolone cheese
1 cup shredded mozzarella cheese
1 quart spaghetti sauce
1 quart tomato juice (needed to swell uncooked noodles)
1/2 cup grated parmesan cheese

In a medium-sized bowl, mix the eggs, ricotta cheese, basil, oregano, and pepper.

Grease the glass baking dish. In the bottom of the dish, spread a few ounces of spaghetti sauce. Place 1 layer of uncooked noodles on the sauce, completely covering the bottom of the dish. Place a layer of zucchini planks on top of the noodles. Using 1/2 of the ricotta and egg mixture, spread the mixture on top of the zucchini. Place 4 slices of provolone cheese over it and spread spaghetti sauce on top. Sprinkle with 1/2 of the mozzarella cheese. Repeat, starting with noodles crossing in the opposite direction of the first layer. When the second layer is complete, carefully pour all of the tomato juice into the lasagna dish, giving it time to soak down between the layers. Sprinkle top of lasagna with the parmesan cheese. Cover tightly with aluminum foil and place in preheated oven for 1 hour. Reduce heat to 300°F and bake for another hour.

Uncover and let stand for 5 to 10 minutes before cutting into squares.

Homemade Ricotta Cheese

We bought our milk at Mashey's Farm. Look for whole organic milk, not ultrapasteurized, for the best results.

Cooking thermometer, cheesecloth (food grade),[1] colander

8 cups whole milk
1 1/2 cups heavy cream
1 teaspoon coarse salt
1/4 cup fresh lemon juice or really good whole cider vinegar

In a large, nonaluminum pot, using a wooden spoon, combine milk, cream, and salt and heat slowly to 195°F over medium heat; this takes about 15 minutes. Add acid (lemon or vinegar) and remove from heat. Let stand about 5 minutes after stirring in the acid.

Line a colander with three layers of cheesecloth and place the colander in a big bowl to catch the whey. Pour cheese into the cloth and let stand 20 minutes for wet cheese or hang for an hour or so for firmer cheese. Keeps 4 days in the refrigerator or you can freeze it.

We like this spread on bread, as a base for dips or baked in a good casserole.

---

[1] Years ago, cheesecloth used to be just that—cloth for making cheese. Now you find "cheesecloth" sold in hardware stores for furniture refinishing. Be careful; it may have chemicals in it from processing! Only use cheesecloth that is food grade; you can find this in better groceries and kitchen supply stores.

Sauces and Relishes

Aunt Orie's Chili Sauce

*I have this recipe from my Aunt Orie, dated 1939. Although a relish,
it is a close relative of ketchup and makes a delicious compliment
to cheeses and cooked meats. It looks really nice in a glass dish.*

Makes 10 cups

10 cups ripe tomatoes, peeled and chopped
1 cup sweet red peppers, chopped fine
3/4 cups onions, chopped fine
1 1/2 tablespoons salt
1/2 cup sugar
1 1/2 cups cider vinegar
1/2 teaspoon cloves
1/2 teaspoon allspice
1/2 teaspoon cinnamon

Wash tomatoes, place in a colander, dip for a few seconds into boiling water, then plunge into cold water. Peel and chop. Put into a good-sized kettle.

Add the other chopped vegetables to the tomatoes. Stir in salt, sugar, and vinegar.

Tie the spices loosely in a bag. Add that bag to the tomato mixture.

Heat and cook down slowly (about 1 or 2 hours) until quite thick, stirring to prevent scorching on the bottom.

Remove spice bag. Place in jars.

Cran Raz Sauce

*This can be a sweet, cool summer spread or a
side dish for your Christmas dinner.*

Makes about 4 cups
6 cups cranberries, fresh or frozen
2 cups red raspberries, fresh or frozen
1 tablespoon lemon juice
5 cups white sugar

Mix all ingredients together in a large, nonaluminum saucepan. Simmer very gently until the cranberries "pop." Allow to cool; process in a food processor until smooth then return to pan.

Bring to a steady boil and cook to jelly stage about 8 minutes or until it sheets off a cool metal spoon.

Pour as much as you want to serve into a pretty crystal dish and refrigerate until serving. Place the rest in a jar in the refrigerator for later use. It also freezes well.

Salsa

You can enjoy this fresh or canned. Follow safe canning directions from your state extension office or a licensed canning cookbook. It also freezes well.

Makes 8–10 quarts

32 cups chopped tomatoes
12 cups finely chopped bell peppers
1/2 to 1 cup finely chopped hot peppers to taste
6 cups finely chopped onions
2 whole heads garlic, peeled and finely minced

Mix the above vegetables together in a large non-reactive container. To save time or to make a less chunky salsa, use a food processor.

To this mixture, add the following:

6 tablespoons chili powder
8 tablespoons cumin
4 tablespoons salt
1 tablespoon black pepper
Juice of 1 lemon
Juice of 1 lime
1/4 cup apple cider vinegar
1/4 cup sugar
Citric acid if canning, following canning directions

Allow the salsa to marry for about 1 hour.

Note: If salsa is very juicy, strain off excess liquid and use it as the liquid to cook rice or beans!

Spaghetti Sauce— from Scratch

This sauce takes three days, but it is worth it! Start with fresh tomatoes or the best canned tomatoes you can find. When you drain the tomatoes, save the juice to drink or to add to soups!

Makes about 5 quarts

20 cups tomatoes, peeled, seeded, and drained

1/4 cup olive oil
1 large onion, coarsely chopped
2 sweet bell peppers, coarsely chopped
1/2 cup fresh garlic, chopped
1/2 cup fresh basil, chopped
1/2 cup fresh parsley, chopped
1/4 cup fresh oregano, or 1 ounce dried
6 tablespoons chili powder
6 tablespoons unsweetened cocoa powder
4 tablespoons salt
2 tablespoons black pepper
2 bay leaves
1 rib of celery
1 1/2 cups red wine, sweet or dry, your choice
2 tablespoons lemon juice

In a large pot, brown the onions and peppers in the olive oil till soft and translucent. Add the garlic, basil, oregano, and parsley. Sauté for a few minutes till fragrant. Add the wine, the lemon juice, and the dry seasonings and continue to stir for a few minutes. Add the tomatoes, bay leaves, and celery last. Simmer very gently for about 2 hours. Cover and let stand overnight at room temperature.

The next day, bring to a low simmer again for 2 hours. If it starts to get too thick or sticks to the pan, add some more wine or tomato juice but not water! If it is not thick enough, you can either continue to simmer or add 1 six-ounce can of tomato paste if you are in a hurry.

Taste the sauce at this point; you can adjust the salt and add a little sugar if you like. Allow the sauce to cool and refrigerate overnight.

The next day, remove the celery rib and the 2 bay leaves. You may leave it "chunky" or put it through a food processor if you like it smooth. Your sauce is ready to enjoy, freeze, or can according to safe canning guidelines.

Vinnie's Pizza Sauce

Whip up this tangy sauce, and if you don't feel like making pizza dough, use it as a dipping sauce for Italian bread!

Makes about 4 cups

32 ounces crushed paste tomatoes, very ripe
2 teaspoons granulated white sugar
4 teaspoons dried oregano
1 teaspoon onion powder or dried onions
1 teaspoon garlic powder (or 1 clove garlic finely minced)
1 teaspoon black pepper
1 teaspoon kosher salt
1 tablespoon olive oil
6 ounces tomato paste (optional)

Put the tomatoes through a tomato strainer or sieve to remove skins and seeds. Mix all ingredients, except tomato paste, in a large non-aluminum pan. Simmer to desired thickness. Add paste as desired to thicken. Adjust garlic and oregano to taste.

Desserts, Candies, Jams, and Confections

Amy's Fabulous Pie Crust
(And How to Assemble a Pie)

This recipe takes a little practice, but once you master this crust, you will become known for your outstanding pies!

9-inch pie pan (I use glass)
Makes 1 crust (top or bottom crust)

Notes:

Make each crust separately; do not double the recipe! It will be too hard to mix, and you may overwork the dough, and it will be tough.

Stale flour will make a tough crust. If your flour has been in your cupboard for more than 3 months, buy new flour for your pie crust. It will be worth it!

The amount of water you use depends on how dry or humid your kitchen is when you are making the crust. The drier the room, the more water it will take. But take care; if you use too much water (and never more than 7 tablespoons), your crust will be pasty and hard.

For 1 crust (top or bottom crust):

1 1/4 cups all-purpose flour, unbleached (very fresh, organic if possible)
1/2 teaspoon salt
1/2 cup best quality salted butter (Amish style, if available), softened to room temperature
5–7 tablespoons ice-cold water

Place flour in pie plate or flat bowl. You can use a flat bowl, but I mix my crust in a 9-inch glass pie pan using a fork.

Drop the salt on top of the flour, then lightly sift the salt into the flour with a fork. Sprinkle the butter in pieces on top of the flour. Cut the butter into the flour/salt mixture working lightly with as few strokes as possible till it is evenly distributed. You will still have some pieces of butter not mixed in completely.

Now sprinkle 5 tablespoons of ice-cold water evenly over your mixture. With the fork, blend in the water with as few strokes as possible. If it does not "come together" into dough quickly, add another tablespoon of ice-cold water and keep trying. The dough should just start to "clean the bowl" and form into a ball. If you make it so wet that it totally cleans the bowl, it is too wet. You can still use it but it will not be special and flaky. If it is very dry in your kitchen, you may have to add the seventh tablespoon of ice-cold water but only if this is necessary to make it hold together enough to roll out.

Place your crumbly ball of dough onto a floured surface, and with a floured rolling pin, roll from the center out till you have an evenly thick round dough a little larger than your pie pan.

Sprinkle it with flour and gently fold it in half, then in half again, then with your hand or a spatula, lift it into your pie pan and unfold it carefully. If you have done everything right, it will want to break and crack. This is good; it means it will be flaky!

Pinch the crust all around the rim of the pan in any design you wish, making sure to crimp it onto the edge of the pan so it will not shrink while baking. If you are going to bake it empty, prick it all over with a fork. Otherwise, fill it with your pie filling right before placing in the oven. Letting it stand even a few minutes full of juicy pie filling will make the bottom crust soggy and tough.

If you are making a two-crust pie, like apple pie, make your 2 separate crusts and roll them out before you mix the filling so it doesn't get too juicy waiting for you. Place the bottom crust in, pour in the filling, lay the top crust on, and crimp both crusts together on the pan edge. Cut slits in the top crust to let steam escape.

Amy's Famous Carrot Cake

*A healthy, heavy, old-fashioned cake. In the early 1980s,
I developed this recipe while looking for healthy treats
for my children. After many decades of being overlooked,
whole wheat was just coming back on the scene.*

2 nine-inch cake pans greased and floured
Preheat oven to 325°F.

1 cup whole wheat flour
1 cup unbleached white flour, or white whole wheat flour
1 cup dark brown sugar
1 teaspoon baking powder
1 teaspoon baking soda
1/4 teaspoon of each: cinnamon, ground clove, nutmeg, ginger and salt
3 cups finely grated carrots
1/4 cup organic molasses
1 cup oil
4 eggs
1/2 cup raisins, plumped in fruit juice
1/2 cup crushed pineapple, drained
1/2 cup chopped walnuts
Grease and flour 2 nine-inch cake pans

In large bowl, combine first 6 ingredients, including all the spices.
Add the next 4 ingredients, stir till combined, then add the last 3.
This batter will be thick and very heavy.

Turn into greased and floured pans and bake at 325°F for 45 to 60 minutes till knife inserted in center comes out clean. Run a knife carefully around the edge of the cake while it is hot and still in the pan. Cool for ten minutes, then remove from pans to cool on a rack.

While it is baking, make cream cheese frosting.

Cream Cheese Frosting

You can decorate the top with walnut halves or pieces of
fruit or drizzle all over with maple syrup or molasses.

8 ounces cream cheese softened
4 ounces (one stick) best-quality, salted butter, softened
2 tablespoons real vanilla extract
2 tablespoons maple syrup
1 cup powdered sugar

For a nice frosting, soften cream cheese and butter. Blend in vanilla extract, maple syrup and powdered sugar. Spread half between the 2 layers and the other half on top. It looks "old-timey" to leave the toasty brown sides of the cake showing.

This cake is good chilled.

Amy's Tea Cakes

As much a sensation as a taste, these cookies disappear in your mouth and from the platter. So special, we only make them for Christmas and Easter. You will want to make them every chance you get. It is imperative to use only real butter and vanilla, fresh unbleached flour, and best quality butter. If you don't, you will get cookies, but you won't have an unforgettable experience.

Makes 4 to 6 dozen, depending on how big you make them
Preheat oven to 325°F.

2 cups real butter
2/3 cup granulated sugar
6 teaspoons real vanilla extract
4 cups unbleached flour
2 cups finely chopped walnuts

Allow the butter to soften at room temperature. Cream together the butter and sugar till smooth. Add the vanilla to the creamed butter and sugar. Be sure to inhale the wonderful fragrance!

Stir in the flour and nuts. Chill the dough for at least 4 hours and up to 24 hours. Any longer than that and the essence of the vanilla will begin to dissipate.

By hand, roll the dough into small balls or logs. Place closely on baking sheets; they do not spread much.

Bake at 325°F for 20 to 40 minutes or till golden brown. Be careful not to burn the bottoms.

Cool to room temperature then roll in powdered sugar till generously coated. Store in airtight containers layered with generous amounts of powdered sugar. They will stay wonderful for several weeks in a cool place. Freezing them diminishes their quality.

Apple Pie

Simple but classic. Don't overdo the cinnamon; let the apple flavor shine through! Use any variety of apple or a mixture of apples, which gives even more depth of flavor.

Apple Pie

Preheat oven to 425°F.
Prepare 2 pie crusts (see "Amy's Fabulous Pie Crust") and set aside; do not roll out till needed.

6 cups apples, peeled and sliced very thin
2 tablespoons lemon juice
1/2 cup sugar
Dash of salt
1/4 teaspoon cinnamon
3 tablespoons white flour

Peel, core, and slice your apples thinly into a large bowl. You should be able to read the newspaper through the apple slices! Sprinkle the apple slices with the lemon juice and toss gently. Set aside.

Roll out 1 of your prepared pie crusts. Drape it in your pie pan loosely. Set aside.

Working quickly, roll out the second crust and leave it lying on the board.

Mix the sugar, salt, cinnamon, and flour into the apples, then immediately pour into the bottom pie crust before the apple juices start to run. Transfer the already rolled-out top crust onto the apples. The pie should be tall and very full. Pinch the crusts together and crimp onto the edge of the pie pan. Use any design you wish to form a pretty rim. Sprinkle white sugar lightly all over the top of the pie. Cut 4 slits in the top of the pie as steam vents.

Place in preheated oven and bake at 425°F for 15 minutes. Reduce heat to 350°F and bake for another 45 minutes. Crust should be golden brown. Test the apples for doneness with a thin knife inserted carefully into the pie through a steam vent. If the apples feel hard, bake for another 10 to 15 minutes at 325°F.

Place on rack to cool.

Blueberry Rhubarb Pie

The name of this pie is a tongue twister, but the flavor is a tongue pleaser. We just call it "blue-barb" pie.

Blueberry Rhubarb Pie

A 9-inch pie pan
Preheat oven to 425°F.

Prepare 2 pie crusts (see "Amy's Fabulous Pie Crust") and set aside; do not roll out till needed.

4 cups rhubarb, washed and sliced into 1/2-inch pieces
2 cups fresh or frozen blueberries thawed
1/2 cup sugar
1/4 teaspoon nutmeg
3 tablespoons white flour

Wash and slice the rhubarb into a large bowl, making sure not to use any leaves. Add the blueberries and toss gently. Set aside.

Roll out 1 of your prepared pie crusts. Drape it in your pie pan loosely. Set aside. Working quickly, roll out the second crust and leave it lying on the board.

Mix the sugar, nutmeg, and flour into the blue-barb filling, then immediately pour into the bottom pie crust before the fruits' juices start to run. Transfer the already rolled-out top crust onto the filling. Pinch the crusts together and crimp onto the edge of the pie pan. Use any design you wish to form a pretty rim. Sprinkle white sugar lightly all over the top of the pie. Cut 4 slits in the top of the pie as steam vents.

Place in preheated oven and bake at 425°F for 15 minutes. Reduce heat to 350°F and bake for another 45 minutes. Crust should be golden brown. If the pie is too pale, bake for another 10 to 15 minutes at 325°F.

Place on rack to cool.

Candy for Decorating Branches

If you read Where the Past is Still Happening, *you might be curious about how Ruth made the candy branches. Here are the recipes she used. You don't have to decorate branches with this candy; simply make the candy, as it is delicious by itself.*

Optional: a few dry, clean tree branches gathered from outside

For Candy (or Decorative "Snow"):

2 cups granulated sugar
1 1/2 cups boiling water
1/8 teaspoon cream of tartar, *or* 2 tablespoons light corn syrup

Butter sides of heavy 1 1/2–quart saucepan. In it combine sugar, water, and cream of tartar (or light corn syrup). Stir over medium heat till sugar dissolves and mixture comes to a boil. Cook without stirring to soft ball stage. (Test for soft ball by dropping a drop of the mixture from your spoon into a glass of cold water and feel it with your finger to see if it is a soft ball. If it dissolves, cook it a little longer and try again.)

Immediately, pour onto a platter and don't scrape the sides of the buttered pan. Cool till the candy feels only warm to the touch. Do not move candy while it cools. Using a wooden spoon, scrape the candy from the edge of the platter toward the center, then work till creamy and stiff. Knead with fingers till free from lumps. At this point proceed as follows:

- If you are making candy branches, drape the candy "snow" on some dry clean branches and drizzle with candy icicles (see recipe below)
- If you are making candy, wrap the candy and place in a container to rest and ripen for 24 hours. After 24 hours, tint, flavor, and shape the candy.

Candy options:

- Peppermints: knead in 10 drops of peppermint extract and 4 drops of organic red or green food coloring.
- Lemon drops: knead in 10 drops lemon extract and 3 or 4 drops organic yellow food coloring.
- Vanilla: knead in 1 tablespoon soft butter and 1 teaspoon vanilla

For the Decorative Candy Branch "Icicles":

1 1/2 cups granulated sugar
2 cups light corn syrup

Make a simple hard candy by mixing the sugar and syrup. Cook over low heat, stirring till the sugar dissolves, about 4 minutes. Cover and cook slowly for 8 more minutes. Uncover and cook to hard ball stage. Cool briefly, then as it thickens and cools, drip it onto your candy branches to look like ice.

My mother didn't have a candy thermometer, but if you have one, feel free to use it. Soft-ball stage is 236°F; hard-ball stage is 250–266°F. Lukewarm is 110°F.

Grandma Ruth's Chocolate Fudge

My mother said, "This is kind of tricky." I think so too, but it is really worth it. The aroma is hypnotic and seems to have therapeutic properties!

Small square cake pan
Makes 2 dozen pieces

2 one-ounce squares unsweetened chocolate, grated
2/3 cup whole milk, scalded
2 cups sugar
1 tablespoon light corn syrup
2 tablespoons butter
1 teaspoon real vanilla extract

In a small saucepan, scald the milk. Butter the sides of another saucepan; melt the chocolate in it slowly without burning. Add the hot, scalded milk. While stirring, add the sugar and the corn syrup. Cook slowly, stirring constantly till the sugar dissolves. Bring to boiling. Cover and cook covered for 3 minutes. Do not permit to boil over. Uncover and cook to soft-ball stage, stirring frequently. (Test for soft ball by dropping a drop of the chocolate mixture from your spoon into a glass of cold water and feel it with your finger to see if it is a soft ball. If it dissolves, cook it a little longer and try again.) Remove from heat.

Add butter; do not stir it in. Cool to lukewarm without stirring. Add vanilla and beat vigorously till the candy is thick and no longer glossy.

Spread in greased pan. Allow to cool completely. When firm, cut into 24 squares.

Notes:

If it doesn't set up, you either didn't cook it to a soft-ball stage or you didn't beat it long enough. Don't throw it away! Use it for hot fudge sundaes! And don't give up; try again till you get it right!

My mother didn't have a candy thermometer, but if you have one, feel free to use it; soft-ball stage is 236°F. Luke-warm is 110°F.

Homemade Pop-Tarts

Need a dessert in a hurry, or a special breakfast addition? These are tasty and fun.

Makes 4 tarts
Preheat oven to 350°F.

> 1 pie crust, prepared rolled out thinly (see "Amy's Fabulous Pie Crust")

Sugar
Any flavor jam or preserves, or softened butter, brown sugar, and cinnamon

Cut the pie crust into 3-inch squares. On half of the squares, generously spread jam to within 1/4 inch of the edge. Moisten the edge with a little bit of water with your finger or a small brush. Place another square of pie crust on top of this and press edges gently together. With a toothpick, prick a few small holes in the top.

Sprinkle with sugar if desired. Alternately, you can make a paste of the butter, sugar, and cinnamon and use it as a filling if you don't have any jam.

Place on ungreased cookie sheet. Bake about 12 to 15 minutes or until golden brown.

Pecan Pie

*Even people who don't love pecan pie declare
this one to be unforgettable.*

A 9-inch pie pan
Preheat oven to 350°F.

1 pie crust, rolled out and placed in pie pan, ready to fill (see "Amy's
Fabulous Pie Crust")
1 1/4 cups whole pecans
2 tablespoons butter
3 eggs, slightly beaten
1 cup brown sugar
1 cup dark corn syrup
2 teaspoons real vanilla extract
2 teaspoons bourbon

In a skillet, fry the pecans in the butter until golden and fragrant.
Set aside.

In a large bowl, combine the eggs, sugar, corn syrup, vanilla, and
bourbon until well blended. Stir in the pecans. Pour into unbaked
pie crust. Bake for 50 to 55 minutes until a knife inserted halfway
between the center and the edge comes out clean. Remove from oven
and cool on a wire rack.

Serve with ice cream or whipped cream.

Pumpkin Pie

This is my favorite pie. You don't have to grow your own pumpkins, but please buy a pumpkin and make this pie from scratch. You will feel connected to the earth and very proud. The resulting pie will be tall and brown with lots of real pumpkin flavor.

Pumpkin Pie

A 9-inch pie pan

To prepare the pumpkin:

Select a pumpkin, medium-sized, about 2 to 3 pounds. Leave it whole, wash it, and prick it around the top with a sharp knife for steam vents. Place the whole pumpkin in a 350°F oven for about 1 hour or till very soft. Remove from oven and allow to cool completely. Remove the skin, cut open gently, and scoop out the seeds. Place the pumpkin flesh in a bowl and mash with a potato masher. I do not puree mine; I like the texture of the pumpkin. You may puree it before you measure for your pie filling if you prefer. If you have leftover pumpkin, it makes a wonderful side dish with butter and cinnamon.

To prepare the pie:

Preheat oven to 425°F.
In a large bowl, mix the following ingredients together with a fork:

16 ounces roasted, peeled, seeded, and mashed pumpkin
12 ounces heavy cream
3 large eggs, slightly beaten
2 tablespoons dark molasses, organic if possible.

In a small bowl, combine the following ingredients and mix well:

3/4 cups brown sugar
1 1/2 tablespoons white flour
1 teaspoon salt
1 teaspoon cinnamon
1/2 teaspoon ginger
1/2 teaspoon nutmeg
1/2 teaspoon ground cloves

When thoroughly blended, add the dry ingredients to the large bowl of wet ingredients. Allow all to marry at room temperature for 30 to 60 minutes.

Prepare a pie crust (see "Amy's Fabulous Pie Crust"), roll it out and place it in your pie pan. When crimping the crust to the edge of the pan, try to leave the crust tall so it will keep the liquid filling in the pan when you move it to the oven.

Pour your filling into the pie crust and place immediately into 425°F oven and bake for 20 minutes. Reduce heat to 350°F and bake for 45 to 50 more minutes or till knife inserted in the middle comes out clean. If it needs to bake a little longer but the crust is getting too brown, reduce heat to 300°F and bake for 10 to 15 more minutes.

Turn oven off when pie is done and crack the oven door slightly. Allow the pie to stand in the cooling oven for 20 minutes. Move to a rack to cool completely. This process should minimize the "fall" of your pie filling as it cools.

Serve with whipped cream, if desired.

Notes: If you want to save the pumpkin seeds to plant next year, cut the raw pumpkin in half and scoop them out before you bake it. Wash the seeds gently in cool water to remove all plant matter and then dry them spread out on a plate or cookie sheet in a cool place away from direct sunlight for 1 week.

Red Raspberry Jam

Pick the berries in the morning before it gets hot out. Make your jam the same day or it will not be as wonderful.

Makes 2 or 3 cups

6 cups red raspberries
6 cups sugar
1 teaspoon lemon juice

Mash berries in a saucepan and stir in the sugar. Cook slowly until the sugar dissolves. Bring quickly to a boil and boil for about 4 to 8 minutes, stirring constantly. Dip a cool spoon into the jam. When it sheets off the spoon, remove immediately from the heat.

Pour into sterilized glass jars. Keep in refrigerator or can according to safe canning practices.

Bernie's Strawberry Jam

This is my father's recipe. Sometimes, when he was very busy picking berries, my father made this jam by placing it in the sun in flat dark-colored roasting pans, very shallow. He covered them with window screens to keep the insects out and let the hot summer sun thicken the jam. Reminiscent of sun-dried tomatoes in concept, but tasting like just-picked berries when served.

Makes about 3 cups

6 cups ripe strawberries
6 cups sugar
1 teaspoon lemon juice

Mash 1/2 of the berries and slice the other 1/2 of the berries. Place all in a saucepan and stir in the sugar. Cook slowly until the sugar dissolves. Bring quickly to a boil and boil 6 minutes, stirring constantly. Dip a cool spoon into the jam. When it is thick and sheets off the spoon, remove immediately from the heat. Do not overcook; it will reduce the flavor.

Pour into sterilized glass jars. Keep in refrigerator or can according to safe canning practices.

Bob's Strawberry Shortcake

What can showcase summer's rubies better than shortcake?

8-inch round cake pan
Makes two-layer cake
Prepare whipped cream.
Preheat oven 425°F. Grease and flour pan.

Wash, slice, mix and set aside:

3 pints fresh strawberries
1/2 cup white sugar

In a medium bowl, mix:

2 1/4 cups unbleached flour
4 teaspoons baking powder
2 tablespoons white sugar
1/4 teaspoon salt

Cut in:
1/3 cup softened butter

Make a well in the center and add:
1 egg, beaten
2/3 cups milk

Stir briefly until just combined.

Spread the batter in the greased and floured pan. Bake at 425°F for 15 to 20 minutes until golden brown. Let cool partially on wire rack, then slice in half making 2 layers. Place 1/2 of the berries and syrup on 1 layer and top with the other layer, cut-side-up. Top with the remaining berries and syrup. Allow cake to soak up the liquid before topping with the whipped cream.

CPSIA information can be obtained
at www.ICGtesting.com
Printed in the USA
BVHW051502020921
615367BV00004B/8